# Management in the Airline Industry

The management of airline pilots is a critically important task for any airline. The impact of industrial action by pilots is immediate and can be extremely costly to the airline, while turnover of flight crew is potentially problematic as civil aviation expands without comparable growth in pilot numbers. Human resource management (HRM) promises to reduce the turnover of pilots and to assuage them from engaging in costly industrial action. Based on original research, this book examines the impact of human resource management on the attitudes of pilots in the UK airline industry.

Prior research has found a positive link between both job satisfaction and organisational commitment, and intention to leave the firm and motivation for work. Advocates claim that HRM increases job satisfaction and organisational commitment among employees. However, HRM remains an ambiguous concept. Drawing on recurrent themes in the literature, this book defines HRM in terms of content (the policies and practices implemented in the workplace) and style (which draws on John Purcell's concept of management style).

Based on data collected from union officials, airline managers, and a large-scale survey of pilots employed at six airlines representative of the UK civil aviation industry, the study finds convergence in the use of HRM content in the management of pilots in UK airlines, but two distinct HRM styles. The data clearly reveal that HRM style is significantly associated with job satisfaction and organisational commitment among the airline pilots surveyed. The data also reveal that commitment both to the organisation and to the union is not only possible for flight crew but more likely than univocal commitment to either the firm or the union. The author also examines pilots' attitudes towards union–management partnership and finds widespread desire for such a partnership in principle, but that in practice desire for partnership was significantly related to the pilots' perception of union effectiveness under partnership.

Of interest to students and academics involved with HRM, the book will also be useful reading for people management practitioners and those with an interest in the aviation industry.

**Geraint Harvey** is Lecturer in Organisational Behaviour and HRM at Swansea University School of Business and Economics.

**Routledge research in employment relations**
Series Editors: Rick Delbridge and Edmund Heery
*Cardiff Business School, UK.*

Aspects of the employment relationship are central to numerous courses at both undergraduate and postgraduate level.

Drawing from insights from industrial relations, human resource management and industrial sociology, this series provides an alternative source of research-based materials and texts, reviewing key developments in employment research.

Books published in this series are works of high academic merit, drawn from a wide range of academic studies in the social sciences.

*Also available from Routledge:*

**Rethinking Industrial Relations**
Mobilisation, collectivism and long waves
*John Kelly*

**Employee Relations in the Public Services**
Themes and issues
*Edited by Susan Corby and Geoff White*

**The Insecure Workforce**
*Edited by Edmund Heery and John Salmon*

**Public Service Employment Relations in Europe**
Transformation, modernisation or inertia?
*Edited by Stephen Bach, Lorenzo Bordogna,
Giuseppe Della Rocca and David Winchester*

**Reward Management**
A critical text
*Edited by Geoff White and Janet Druker*

**Working for McDonald's in Europe**
The unequal struggle?
*Tony Royle*

**Job Insecurity and Work Intensification**
*Edited by Brendan Burchell, David Ladipo and
Frank Wilkinson*

**Union Organizing**
Campaigning for trade union recognition
*Edited by Gregor Gall*

**Employment Relations in the Hospitality and
Tourism Industries**
*Rosemary Lucas*

# Management in the Airline Industry

## Geraint Harvey

LONDON AND NEW YORK

First published 2007
by Routledge
2 Park Square, Milton Park, Abingdon, Oxfordshire OX14 4RN

Simultaneously published in the USA and Canada
by Routledge
711 Third Avenue, New York, NY 10017

First issued in paperback 2014

*Routledge is an imprint of the Taylor and Francis Group, an informa business*

© 2007 Geraint Harvey

Typeset in Times by Wearset Ltd, Boldon, Tyne and Wear

*British Library Cataloguing in Publication Data*
A catalogue record for this book is available from the British Library

*Library of Congress Cataloging in Publication Data*
A catalog record for this book has been requested

ISBN13: 978-0-415-39078-1 (hbk)
ISBN13: 978-0-415-75940-3 (pbk)

To my wife, Claire, and in memory of
my mother, Glynis

# Contents

# Illustrations

## Figures

## Tables

# Acknowledgements

The publication of this book would not have been possible without the contribution of family, colleagues (past and present), and friends.

Immeasurable gratitude is due to my grandmother, Betty, father, Keith, brother, Lindsay, and wife, Claire, for their boundless enthusiasm and constant support.

I am extremely grateful to Peter Turnbull, who supervised the research and writing of the original thesis on which this book is based and was instrumental in the development of the book. Without his guidance and patient sagacity this book would never have been produced.

The sponsorship of the Economic and Social Research Council (Award PTA-026–27–0270 and R42200034178) is also gratefully acknowledged.

The author is most appreciative of the permission granted by the European Cockpit Association (and Europairs) and Barbara Cassani (and Time Warner/Little Brown Book Group) to use extracts from their publications.

Thanks are also due to:

Paul Blyton, John Doyle, Ed Heery, John Purcell, Alan Watkins, Karen Williams, and Andy Henley, for their contribution to the evolution and expression of ideas conveyed.

Rob Hall, Bob Carton, John Moore, and especially John McGurk whose interest and patronage ensured the success of the research project.

Colleagues from Cardiff Business School and the Swansea University School of Business and Economics, namely Michael Marinetto, Peter Samuel, Christina Volkmann, and Christian De Cock and the informal Cardiff Business School 'social society', whose support and friendship have been invaluable throughout the (lengthy) period of preparation.

Ryan 'Softy' David and the HOPA (Jason 'Larry' Lawrence, 'Big' Richard Evans, Darren 'DH' Holland, Chris 'Chick' Jones, Steffan 'Biler' Jones, Noel 'Laser' Thomas, John Deakin, Jas Garrens, Ed Dodd and the rest), for all the giggles.

Sharon and Jack; Rose, Amy, and Charlie; Nick, Hilary, Sarah, Sam, Richard, Ruth, and John, Rhiannon, and Nigel, Brett and Zanna, Neil, and Leo, Dave and Zoe, Chris, Becky, and anyone else I've missed (sorry!) ...

Cheers.

# Abbreviations

| | |
|---|---|
| AMO | ability, motivation, and opportunity |
| ANOVA | analysis of variance |
| ATKs | available tonne kilometre |
| AWP | alternative work practices |
| BA | British Airways |
| BALPA | British Air Line Pilots Association |
| bmi | British Midland International |
| CAA | Civil Aviation Authority |
| CRF | commitment regression factor |
| CRM | crew resource management |
| ECA | European Cockpit Association |
| ESOP | Employee Stock Ownership Plan |
| HRM | human resource management |
| IATA | International Air Transport Association |
| ICAO | International Civil Aviation Organisation |
| IiP | Investors in People |
| ILO | International Labour Organisation |
| ITF | International Transport Workers Federation |
| KSA | knowledge, skills, and abilities |
| OLS | ordered least squares |
| TQM | total quality management |

# 1 Introduction

This book examines the management of people in the airline industry. More specifically, it focuses on the management of pilots in the UK airline industry and the impact that human resource management (HRM) has upon their attitudes towards their airline and their work. It is based on a study of flight crew, sponsored by the Economic and Social Research Council (ESRC) and conducted between 2001 and 2005. A study of airline pilots is timely. Despite the crucial importance of competent flight crew management (discussed at length in Chapter 2), the last major study of pilots in the UK was carried out in the late 1960s by A.N.J. Blain.[1] Pilots then, as now, enjoy(ed) considerable industrial strength. Consequently, any collective expression of discontent, such as threatened industrial action, can cost an airline dearly (e.g. the threat of industrial action by pilots in BA in 1996 cost the airline an estimated £15 million). At airlines that operate the seniority rule, which binds pilots to one airline as they accrue non-transferable benefits, pilots must resort to *voicing* any discontent,[2] which they are frequently prone to do in an adversarial manner,[3] because they are effectively prevented from *exiting* the airline. In this context, pilots' attitudes can be crucial to the survival of the airline. As exit is a more likely strategy for pilots employed at airlines that do not operate a seniority rule, therein management is confronted with the problem of pilot retention. As later chapters show, the growth of civil aviation has not been matched by a growth in pilot numbers and there has been widespread concern about a shortage of flight crew to meet demand. In this environment, pilot retention is a fundamental objective of management. Finally, pilots are among the highest-paid employees in any airline. With the necessity for airlines to reduce employee costs,[4] the management of pilots is fraught with difficulties.

HRM offers airline management a potential 'solution' to these problems. Advocates claim that HRM engenders feelings of satisfaction with work and commitment to the organisation, thereby reducing intentions to leave and the propensity for recourse to industrial action. A promise like this is no doubt appealing to the beleaguered flight operations manager, especially when the literature is replete with HRM success stories drawn from civil aviation, for example British Airways (BA),[5] Delta Airlines,[6] Lufthansa,[7] Singapore Airways,[8] and, of course, Southwest Airlines.[9]

The lion's share of HRM research throughout the 1990s investigated the correlation between the presence of HRM and the performance of the firm,[10] rather than its impact on employees.[11] As a result of the problems in demonstrating the link between HRM and firm performance directly, research has been refocused to examine the impact of HRM on the attitudes of employees towards their work. For example, the recent Bath People and Performance model posits that HRM increases the ability of the employee to do the job; motivates the employee to go the extra mile for the firm; and offers the employee the opportunity to demonstrate enhanced ability and motivation.[12] It was usually assumed, rather than demonstrated, that HRM policies and practices led to higher levels of employee motivation and commitment to the firm.[13] The analyses of the impact of HRM on the attitudes of employees that emerged at the very end of the twentieth century and into the new millennium offered far from conclusive findings.[14]

In a bid to explain the variation in findings, the focus of research has extended beyond the actual policies and practices implemented by the firm to variables that moderate the impact of the policies and practices, such as the process of HRM implementation.[15] There is a tradition of conceptualising HRM in terms of elements other than tangible practices. In the early 1990s, Schuler categorised five components of HRM.[16] Within this framework one component stands out: the HR philosophy, which is described as the guidelines about 'how the organization regards its human resources, what role the resources play in the overall success of the business, and how they are to be treated and managed'.[17] The notion of an overarching philosophy, which is the 'moral foundation' of the firm or 'company culture', is found in Pfeffer's slightly later iteration.[18] Most recently, in their comprehensive account of strategic HRM, Boxall and Purcell identify the underpinning layer of HRM, described as generic processes and general principles, which guides HR and indeed general employee relations activity within the firm.[19] This theme permeates Purcell's thinking on employee relations, from the notion of 'good industrial relations'[20] through 'management style'[21] to underpinning HRM and the Bath People and Performance Model that highlights the necessity for management to generate a conducive environment of trust, encouragement and respect in order for other aspects of HRM, namely HRM policies and practices, to 'work'.[22]

In this book, HRM is presented as comprised of two components, which roughly equate to Boxall and Purcell's surface and underpinning layers of HRM.[23] They describe the surface layer as consisting of the policies and practices implemented by the firm in the management of people. These policies and practices are labelled the content of HRM in this book as they represent the readily measurable component of HRM. The philosophy and processes of HRM, otherwise known as the underpinning layer of HRM, build on Purcell's concept of 'management style'. The second component of HRM as distinguished in this book is closely aligned with Purcell's 'management style', but differs in some very important ways (see Chapter 3). Therefore, the label of HRM style is used. HRM style is expressed in management attitude and action towards employees as individuals (individualism), whereas collectivism in HRM style concerns the approach of management towards collective representation.

A primary aim of the study on which this book is based was to examine the relative impact of the two broad dimensions of HRM content and style on the attitudes of employees, airline pilots in this case.

The collective dimension of HRM style introduces another significant stakeholder group, the trade union, whose relationship with HRM is extremely important.[24] The way in which management deal with trade unions is seen as reflecting collectivism in HRM style. This book avers that a genuine union–management partnership occurs when cooperative collectivism in HRM style is matched by a moderate approach on the part of the trade union, for the purpose of achieving mutual gains. The study was also able to assess the attitudes of pilots towards the 'new realism' of the workplace.[25]

The contribution of this study goes beyond facilitating our understanding of the way in which pilots in the UK are managed. More than this, it addresses two very important issues in employment relations. First, this study explores pilots' attitudes towards work and clearly delineates the impact of HRM content and HRM style. Second, the impact of HRM on the trade union has been discussed widely and has generated numerous empirical studies in the UK. However, these have focused on the implications for trade unions and the outcomes for employees, such as job losses and wage reduction.[26] Research has only recently considered the views of members towards partnership or towards their union after it had embraced partnership. This study evaluates desire for partnership in principle, among pilots at non-partnership airlines, and desire for partnership in practice, among flight crew at the two airlines with which the pilots' trade union, the British Air Line Pilots Association (BALPA), had engaged management in partnership at the time of study.

So that the research could best address the agenda identified above, attitudinal data were collected from a representative sample of unionised pilots at six airlines operating in the UK civil aviation industry, specifically the full-service airlines BA and bmi (British Midland International); easyJet and Go of the low-cost sub-sector; and the charter airlines Britannia and Air2000. BALPA representatives employed at each of the six sample airlines participated in focus groups conducted during BALPA Company Council Industrial Forums at the Association head office. Pilots and management employed at two of the airlines, easyJet and BA, were interviewed along with all senior officials at BALPA. A comprehensive questionnaire survey was distributed to a census of all flight crew who were members of BALPA and employed at all airlines in the sample other than BA. A stratified random sample comprised of one-third of BA-employed BALPA members also received the questionnaire. The response rate to the questionnaire at each of the airlines exceeded 25 per cent.

Whereas the airlines in the sample were operating with very different business strategies, the data show that pilots employed at the six airlines experienced very similar HRM policies and practices. These findings indicate convergence on HRM content among airlines in the UK. This is not surprising as each of the three pressures for isomorphism[27] (coercive, mimetic, and normative) is widespread in the UK civil aviation industry. An alternative way of describing this situation, which has more currency in the HRM literature, is to suggest that in the management of pilots, the 'table stakes'[28] are very high.

Despite experiencing the same HRM policies and practices, the levels of job satisfaction and organisational commitment reported by pilots differed significantly between airlines. In the low-cost and charter sub-sectors, pilots employed at Go (low-cost sub-sector) and Britannia (charter sub-sector) were significantly more likely to report positive attitudes, whereas pilots employed at easyJet (low cost), and Air2000 (charter) were significantly more likely to be negative.

At Go and Britannia, the HRM style towards flight crew reflected cooperative collectivism and high individualism. At easyJet and Air2000, HRM style towards flight crew was marked by adversarial collectivism and low individualism. The data reveal that in contrast to convergence on HRM content, two very different HRM styles were apparent. Multivariate data analysis reveals that the HRM style pursued by airline management was strongly associated with pilots' attitudes towards work. There was, however, no such nexus between the attitudes of pilots and of HRM content.

There are several reasons why pilots might favour partnership between BALPA and airline management (these are discussed fully in Chapter 8), and why pilots are more likely to be satisfied in their work and committed to the airline where management pursues cooperative collectivism. Unsurprisingly then, pilot response to the principle of the union adopting a cooperative approach towards airline management was very positive, with over three-quarters of respondents agreeable to a hypothetical partnership. However, at the two airlines where BALPA had, at the time of the study, engaged management in partnership, desire for partnership among flight crew differed significantly. Between these airlines, there was also a more extreme variation in pilot perception of union efficacy. The powerful association between perceived union efficacy and desire for partnership illustrates the widespread popularity of partnership in practice where the union was perceived to remain effective under partnership. The data show that partnership in practice must deliver, as desire was considerably less widespread where the union was perceived to have lost leverage.

## Structure of the book

The subsequent chapters elaborate on this synopsis. Chapter 2 portrays the context of the civil aviation industry and the peculiarities of the work of airline pilots. Chapter 3 considers the HRM literature and emphasises the need to research the analytical distinction between the components of HRM. This chapter also presents a brief synopsis of the partnership debate and considers the arguments and evidence on the outcomes of such an arrangement. Chapter 4 outlines the study, discussing the methods employed in the collection of data and the techniques used in their analysis. Chapter 5 first assesses the content of HRM at the airlines and then explores the style adopted by airlines towards flight crew and BALPA. Chapter 6 considers the extent of job satisfaction among pilots at the six airlines. Data concerning overall job satisfaction and satisfaction with aspects of work are analysed in an approach consistent with previous job satisfaction research, and the effect of HRM content and style is assessed. Chapter 7 features the analysis of organisational commitment and measures the impact of HRM content and style. This chapter also explores the relationship between organisational commitment and commitment to the union and finds a strong positive relationship between these diverse and, some would argue, antithetical forms of commitment. Chapter 8 reports the response of pilots to partnership in principle and partnership in practice. Chapter 9 summarises the key findings of the research and discusses the implications for airline management and BALPA.

# 2   Civil aviation and the airline pilot

## Introduction

This book examines the management of people in the airline industry, specifically focusing on the impact of human resource management (HRM) on the attitudes of airline pilots. There has been a dearth of HRM research in the service sector[1] despite its expansion and importance in the global economy.[2] Civil aviation is arguably among the most significant and fastest-growing areas in the service sector. In a keynote address to the World Civil Aviation Chief Executives Forum, the President of the International Civil Aviation Organisation (ICAO), Roberto Gonzalez, quoted the following statistics illustrating this growth: scheduled traffic grew from eight million passengers in 1945 to two billion in 2005 and this figure was anticipated to rise to approximately three billion by 2015. The industry provides in excess of 28 million jobs for the world's workforce and $1360 billion in annual gross output.[3] Its ramifications for the wider economy were discussed by Mr Gonzalez who commented that 'every $100 of output produced and every 100 jobs generated by air transportation trigger additional demands of some $325 and 610 jobs in other industries'.[4] Civil aviation is also intriguing because of the peculiarities of the industry, which make people management especially difficult. Management of airline pilots is a particularly exacting endeavour. Airline pilots are atypical of the majority of the employees in an airline. They possess substantial industrial power in comparison with other airline workers due to their non-substitutability, the immediate impact of any industrial action on their part, and the extremely tight labour market for pilots with commercial experience. The unusual nature of the industry and employee focus of the research require further elaboration. This chapter, therefore, presents a discussion of the peculiarities of the work of the airline pilot and the idiosyncrasies of the civil aviation industry.

## The airline pilot

> Briefly the two extreme points of view are (a) that an airline pilot is a
> kind of demi-god, a hero of the air combining the gallantry and
> resource of a fighter pilot who has won the Victoria Cross with the
> skill and judgment and navigational ability of the Captain of an
> Atlantic liner and (b) that he is a glorified bus-driver. The truth, as in
> all violent argument, lies somewhere between the two extremes.[5]

This quote, taken from the last major study focused entirely on the management of flight crew in the UK some 40 years ago,[6] conveys an enduring
dissonance of perspective that is relevant to the industry today. As this
book will show, the treatment of pilots at several airlines in the UK
emphasises their skills and technical contribution, whereas others have
unwittingly perpetuated view (b) in the quotation above. For example, the
effervescent Chairman of easyJet, Stelios Haji-Ioannou, stated emphati-
cally of the airline that, 'We're a bus company'.[7] Many pilots at the airline
felt that they were seen as bus drivers by implication. In addition, the
flight deck has become increasingly automated and pilots feel their status
has been devalued. Simon Bennett, author of *A Sociology of Commercial
Flight Crew*, writes,

> there is a feeling that, with today's highly automated glass cockpits,
> pilots are being disempowered and deskilled to the point where they
> may become a liability … . It remains to be seen whether the shift in
> the 'balance of power' between pilot-craftsman and technologist will
> have any long-term implications for the profession.[8]

Despite the apparent deskilling of pilots, it is generally accepted that
flight crew are fundamental to civil aviation. One cynical management
participant in the present study quipped that pilots were necessary 'if only
because their presence reassures the customer' (*Interview notes*).

Diminishing status aside, pilots also face an impending assault on
traditional employment relations. In 2003, the Director General of the
International Air Transport Association (IATA), Giovanni Bisignani,
announced at an IATA annual general meeting that: '[Pilots] must not
hide behind old work rules, such as seniority lists, which are out of touch
with today's competitive world. This industry needs to reward performance, not age or seniority'.[9] Such an approach has been taken in the management of pilots by low-cost carriers. A significant proportion of the
low-cost airline pilot's salary is dependent upon performance (number of
routes flown) and pilots are expected to perform to the very limit of legal

flight time. Like other employee groups in the industry,[10] pilots have faced major challenges to their traditional work routines in recent years.[11]

The management of civil aviation pilots is complicated by two features of their work: their substantial industrial power and the disincentive for a pilot to leave an airline. A suitable framework for assessing the level of power an industrial group wields has been presented by the industrial sociologist, Erik Olin Wright,[12] who measures power along structural and associational dimensions. Structural power, he argues, derives from 'the location of workers within the economic system'.[13] Sources of structural power are the tightness of the labour market for the particular employee group and their strategic importance to the business. Flight crew score highly on these criteria. First, the tightness of the labour market is demonstrated by the current shortage of pilots in Europe and indeed across the globe,[14] the consequences of which have begun to emerge.[15] In a recent high-profile discrimination case, senior flight operations management at BA blamed a pilot shortage for their refusal to allow a female co-pilot, Jessica Starmer, to work part-time hours.[16] In order to meet this shortfall, airlines have petitioned to raise the retirement age of pilots and ICAO has proposed the introduction of Multi-Crew Pilot Licences, which would reduce the cost and time necessary to train pilots. However, this proposal has met with staunch resistance from pilots' associations on the grounds that it would lead to a diminution of safety. It has also been viewed as yet further evidence of the deskilling of the flight crew profession.

Second, pilots occupy a strategic position of paramount importance to airlines. As Johnson observes, flight crew are highly skilled and possess extensive generic and specific knowledge that makes their replacement in a strike virtually impossible.[17] Currently, the British Air Line Pilots Association (BALPA) calculates the cost of obtaining a Private Pilot's Licence as approximately £6000. The process can take 6–12 months to complete. The cost of gaining the qualification which enables the pilot to fly in instrument conditions is a further £2000, and in order to fly at night a further cost of £750 is accrued.[18] These qualifications enable the pilot to 'fly for fun' but not for 'hire or reward'. In order to earn money as a pilot, a Commercial Pilot's Licence must be obtained. This course will take between nine and 36 months at a cost of £50,000–60,000, although full and partial scholarships are available from some UK airlines.[19] Presently, in order to gain a commercial pilot's licence, the pilot must have 700 hours' flying experience, together with the successful completion of the Air Law examination and an Instrument Rating Flight Test.[20]

In contrast, cabin crew can be trained from novice to operational standard in four weeks, as BA demonstrated during the cabin crew strike of 1997 when replacement staff were drafted into an army barracks and intensively trained to replace striking employees.[21] A similar strategy is considerably more difficult with regard to airline pilots. BA's public response to the threatened pilot strike in 1996, importing crews to fly its routes, was made a laughing stock in the media. As Chris Darke, former General Secretary of BALPA, pointed out:

> You just cannot take a pilot off one 747 operated by a foreign opera-tor, wheel them over and stick them into BA and say 'Fly that'. It just doesn't work like that. There are all sorts of standard operating proce-dures that the airline has in place which the pilot has to operate to. There are route checks. There are a whole series of induction arrange-ments that would be necessary to get anybody in the cockpit. It was a complete nonsense.
>
> *(Interview notes*, August 2001)

Whereas the 1997 cabin crew dispute was costly for BA (see below), the airline was able to develop a contingency plan to replace militant workers. This contingency was and is not feasible for flight crew.

The second power dimension identified by E.O. Wright, associational power, is a function of collective organisation coordinated most usually by trade unions. Flight crew are highly unionised in those airlines where BALPA has been historically recognised for collective bargaining, for example BA, Britannia Airlines, and bmi. In excess of 70 per cent of pilots at bmi and above 80 per cent at both BA and Britannia Airlines were members of BALPA at the time the study was conducted. In those airlines where BALPA has achieved recognition recently union membership varied from around 40 per cent to 70 per cent. High union density in most of the airlines is accompanied by a readiness to impose industrial action. For example, industrial action was threatened by BALPA in 2004, on behalf of its membership in response to the introduction of new laws harmonising flying hours across the European Union; and in 2006, on behalf of its bmi members in response to failed pay negotiations,[22] on behalf of its BA members in response to potential changes to the final salary pension scheme,[23] and on behalf of its members employed at bmibaby over a pay dispute. Aside from these instances, officials at the Association claimed that similar threats had been narrowly averted at several other airlines.

The propensity for industrial action among flight crew is interesting given the socio-economic origins of the majority of pilots and the image they wish to convey. Bennett[24] notes that pilots are most likely to have been born into middle- or upper-middle-class households and thus might be expected to hold moderate views on industrial action. Also, moderation might be expected because of their desire to be recognised as professionals and for BALPA to be acknowledged as a professional association. This peculiar incongruity of the pilot's character was captured succinctly by the *Independent* reporter Chris Wolmar. In a report about the threatened industrial action by pilots at BA in 1996, he records an incident between then General Secretary Chris Darke and a BALPA representative:

> One pilot coming out of a meeting harangued Chris Darke, BALPA's general secretary, saying 'Don't sell us out. We are rock solid about this'. Mr Darke, taken aback, said 'You are behaving like Trots', and then said 'sorry, you won't understand that', having realised that a pilot was likely to think a 'Trot' had something to do with his daughter's pony.[25]

Whereas pilots are conservative and fiercely defensive of both their professional status[26] and the role of BALPA as a professional association, they are quite prepared for BALPA to behave unlike other professional associations, such as the British Medical Association, in threatening industrial action if necessary. Thus the pilot represents an interesting paradox, wishing to be treated as a professional while concomitantly prepared to resort to pugilism.

As the product of the airline cannot be stockpiled, and a threat of action alone can reduce passenger bookings, as demonstrated at BA in 1996 when the threat of industrial action by BALPA cost BA an estimated £15 million in advance bookings, the pilot wields significant bargaining power.[27] In separate interviews with a flight operations manager at BA and with Chris Darke of BALPA, both agreed that the industrial power of the pilot is 'absolute'. As Chris Darke put it: 'I'm not saying that other groups of people can't effect by strike, influence over their employer, but there aren't many that can have that immediate, absolute effect. Pilots can' (*Interview notes*, August 2001).

Expressing their discontent in this way can have a considerable negative impact on the profitability of an airline, and in airlines that operate a seniority clause this may be the only recourse for the disgruntled pilot. Cappelli[28] writes of the US airline industry that pilots are economically restricted from pursuing alternative forms of employment or employment with alternative carriers. First, he notes that the skills learned and utilised by airline pilots have little or no transferability to any employment other than flying aircraft. More importantly perhaps, no alternative employment would offer a similar salary. Second, citing the binding power of seniority rules, Cappelli claims that movement of pilots between carriers is also limited as such transfers result in a loss of seniority, with consequent loss of roster privileges and a sharp pay cut.

Although the seniority clause rewards loyal service, it also restricts pilots from seeking career progression with other airlines and limits their response to perceived unfair treatment. Unable to vote with their feet, the *exit* response is eliminated, leaving them with only the ability to express their *voice*.[29] This means that industrial action is often the only feasible option left open to the dissatisfied airline pilot. Unwilling to leave the airline, the pilot will often seek to impose sanctions on the firm. But operating without the seniority clause presents its own problem.

The seniority clause seriously curtails pilot inter-airline mobility. As such it allows airlines to invest in pilots without the fear of losing them to a competitor soon after completing the training and thus wasting a considerable sum of money. This point was emphasised by the current General Secretary of BALPA, Jim McAuslan, in response to the comments made by IATA Director General Bisignani concerning the need to remove seniority benefits for pilots (see above). McAuslan pointed out that without seniority the airline pilot would become an incredibly valuable and mobile commodity, especially as a dire pilot shortage is anticipated by the European Cockpit Association (ECA).[30] While the seniority rule exists, pilots are at least bound to the airline and management can depend on their labour. However, if seniority is removed, as is the case in easyJet, the effective management of pilots will become considerably more, not less, important. Without the seniority rule, pilots will be free to express their *exit* response, leave an airline and offer their labour either to the highest bidder or the 'best' employer. And the best employer might not necessarily be perceived as the one offering the highest remuneration. Migration of flight crew to a preferred employer is distinctly probable, as has been proved at easyJet, where flight crew turnover was estimated at around 10 per cent in 2004, more than double that of any other UK airline at the time (*Interview notes*, February 2004).

The situation may be aggravated in future years if the pilot shortage anticipated by ECA materialises. Airline management will not have access to a labour market sufficient to adopt a 'take it or leave it' attitude to their flight crew. There simply will not be the labour source available upon which to draw. At the time of A.N.J. Blain's study, the attraction of a career in civil aviation as a pilot was already dissipating. The situation has arguably been exacerbated in the 30 years since Blain's study, as a Senior First Officer explained of the situation at their airline:

> We have no life; days off are spent recovering from deep/long night flights, and precede 4 am reports. Completely irregular patterns mean we are often going to work when the previous day we were going home at the same time! Crew are so tired we can hardly even keep our eyes open even when on the runway at takeoff. Passengers have no idea, and would be horrified if they heard what we do.

I spent, in real terms, £80,000 to train to fly. I'm seriously thinking about leaving aviation. The financial reward does not compensate for feeling permanently tired, stressed, and fed up with the company ... I wouldn't recommend this job to anyone. If I could turn back the clock and not do it, I would!

(QRN 266)[31]

Sentiments such as these were common among pilots who were surveyed and indeed reflect the findings of other studies of flight crew. Bennett reports at length complaints by pilots about the detrimental impact of their work on family and social life.[32]

Aside from collective industrial action, the dissatisfied airline pilot might also impose sanctions at an individual level. For example, a pilot might decide to carry extra fuel which leads to considerable wastage and cost (carrying 500 kg of fuel wastes 20 kg per hour in extra burn). As in many other jobs, work-to-rule is a constant threat to management. One interviewee illustrated the way in which pilots demonstrate discretionary effort – effort that can legitimately be withdrawn should they feel aggrieved by their treatment:

Once people are de-motivated by their perceived treatment by the management they stop being company-minded ... 'work-to-rule' is definitely an option. There are plenty of areas where we regularly help the company out in order to get the job done, all of which would create delays if we played things strictly by the rules. For instance, report time is departure minus one hour, but we normally arrive well before this in order to cope with IT problems and reading the large number of NOTAMS [Notice to Airmen] ... and to allow for traffic delays of course. If we reported on time and insisted on briefing properly, as required by law, we'd be late. Unforeseen delays during the day can mean going into discretion, exceeding the allowed flight duty period at the discretion of the commander. Refusing to do this is an easy option, requiring crews to be called out from standby.

(*Interview notes*, October 2005)

The competent management of pilots is evidently an important and a fraught endeavour, whether management aim to retain pilots where the seniority rule is absent, or whether industrial action must be prevented where pilots are bound to the airline. The management of people in the airline more generally is complicated by three 'peculiarities' of civil aviation. These concern the product of civil aviation, the pro-cyclical demand for air transport, and both the proportion and the variability of labour costs.[33]

## Perishable product, pro-cyclical demand and proportion of labour costs

The product of air transport is highly perishable. If flights are cancelled, airlines cannot easily recover lost traffic in the immediate future. The protracted cabin crew dispute at BA in 1997 is estimated to have cost the airline in excess of £125 million, while the dispute at the airline in July 2003, involving a 24-hour walkout staged by customer service and check-in staff, resulted in five days of delays affecting up to 80,000 passengers and costing the airline an estimated £40 million.[34] Although revenue may be recouped from passengers who defer their trip and then fly with the same airline, more serious events will have a more significant and longer-term negative impact on passenger confidence and loyalty. The latter situation can create a 'vicious spiral' of traffic losses, followed by price reductions in order to win back passengers which then necessitate a higher load factor in order for the airline to break even. Further price reductions may be offered in order to raise the aircraft load, but these price reductions make profitability ever more elusive. With so high a price to pay for industrial disruption, airline management are arguably courting disaster if they neglect employee relations.

Aside from exogenous events such as industrial disruption and war, demand for air transport is pro-cyclical. Air traffic expands (contracts) with increased (decreased) economic growth *but at a much faster rate*. The cycle of peak and trough results in the expectations of management and labour being out of sync. This dichotomy of perception is at its widest at the peak of the cycle, when demand is at its zenith. To the front-line employee, such as check-in staff, cabin crew, and flight crew, a full aircraft means the airline is performing well enough for management to compensate them for previous sacrifices made during the last trough. But in anticipation of the next trough, management may choose to remain cautious with the airline's finances, refusing demands by employees for improved remuneration. Advanced bookings are routinely compared with previous periods, enabling management to predict falling demand before employees witness any reduction in 'bums on seats'. As Doganis comments, management has been able to persuade employees to accept reduced terms and conditions in times of crisis. It is quite a different matter to gain similar concessions based on an *anticipated* downturn in demand:

> when airlines are profitable, and things are going well, employees rightly want to share in the profits generated. It is difficult to persuade them that a new crisis is impending as a result of intensified competition and that to avoid future losses and an airline's possible collapse it is essential for them to make sacrifices now.[35]

A potential outcome of this dissonance between the perspectives of management and of the employee is deterioration in employment relations or even industrial conflict.

Finally, labour accounts for around 30 per cent of a traditional airline's operational costs and is one of the few variable costs in the industry under the direct and more immediate control of management. Labour has become the largest single cost element and a major factor differentiating one airline's cost from another's.[36] In the competitive environment of the civil aviation industry of the twenty-first century cost reduction strategies are necessarily ubiquitous and constant, and inevitably focus on reducing labour costs.[37] Pilot wages account for a disproportionate total of airlines' labour costs. In 2002, pilots comprised less than 7 per cent of total employees at BA, but accounted for around 19 per cent of labour costs.[38] Thus, Doganis asserts that 'controlling pilot salaries is so critical for airlines and … negotiating an agreement with pilots is a key part of any airline's labour relations'.[39] In the UK, this is especially true of BA. Whereas pilot salaries account for a disproportionate amount of labour costs within the airline, the average salary of BA pilots is among the lowest in Europe, the US, and Asia.[40] Doganis notes that pilots have no counterparts within their own airline and consequently no group against which to assess the equity of their salaries. Instead, pilots compare their salaries with those of pilots at 'comparable' airlines. For BA, the UK flag carrier, comparable airlines would be other European flag carriers such as Lufthansa, Air France, and Scandinavian Air Services, where the average pilot salaries are considerably higher.[41]

Clearly, then, these facets of the industry influence the way in which employees generally, and pilots specifically, are managed. The competitive environment has also changed in the UK civil aviation industry since the late 1980s as a result of the gradual liberalisation of the European civil aviation industry. An effect of liberalisation was the greater degree to which airline management could intensify the globalisation of airline product and labour markets. A report commissioned by ECA illustrates how the consequent environment provides airline management with both the *motive* and the *opportunity* to restructure the work of its employees in order to elicit enhanced productivity and efficiency.[42]

## Liberalisation and globalisation

In Europe, the civil aviation industry began a process of liberalisation in 1987:

> Undertaken through a 10-year, three-phase programme, the process did away with the old system where schedules, fares and passenger

numbers had been largely controlled by bilateral agreements between European nations. As a result, since 1997 any airline holding a valid air operator's certificate (AOC) in the EU can fly any route within the region, including services entirely within another country.[43]

The less regulated environment permitted the established carriers to evolve in domestic and foreign markets (in effect propelling globalisation of civil aviation) and encouraged a host of new entrant airlines to compete with the established airlines. In the early 1980s, the largest carrier in the UK, BA, was privatised. With the exception of US carriers, state ownership was common among the world's largest airlines. These airlines had enjoyed preferential access to their host country's major airports and had also been afforded 'sovereignty', with the host government severely restricting entry into the market in order to limit competition with the flag carrier.[44] Pre-liberalisation, British Caledonian was the only airline to emerge to compete with BA in the UK. Bilateral agreements between countries also determined routes, frequency of service and fares charged, effectively eliminating price competition between flag carriers. Thus, prior to privatisation, there was little incentive for the flag carrier to improve service quality or efficiency because of the closed product market.[45] Responsible to shareholders and subject to increased competition, the firm had to evolve.

Doganis identifies three features of BA global strategy after privatisation and during liberalisation: 'dominate your home market, ensure a presence in the other major European markets and establish a global spread through alliances with US Asian/Pacific carriers'.[46] BA acquired a large share of its largest competitor, British Caledonian, and many of the smaller domestic and European carriers operating from the UK, e.g. Dan-Air, CitiFlyer Express, and Maersk. Internationally, BA acquired shares in the German domestic carrier, Delta Air, and in both TAT and Air Liberté in France. Meanwhile the European flag carriers SAS and Lufthansa sought influence in the UK by purchasing shares in the largest airline independent of BA influence, bmi.

The globalisation of the airline product market has also involved an expansion of route networks and the establishment of strategic alliances such as **one**world, involving BA, and the Star Alliance, in which British Midland International (bmi) is a partner. In 2003, the Star Alliance revenues exceeded $80 billion, the partners operated 2140 aircraft, employed over 282,000 staff, and serviced 342 million passengers. Similarly, the revenue of the **one**world alliance partners exceeded $50 billion, operated 1600 aircraft, employed 245,000 employees and carried 209 million passengers.[47] The globalisation of labour markets has occurred through 'out-basing' whereby airline employees are based in different parts of the world, often on worse terms and conditions than their home-based colleagues. Alternatively, airlines have relocated aspects of the business to low-wage economies to take advantage of the lower wages and social charges incurred in these countries. The global expansion of the airline labour market is illustrated by BA relocating its ticket processing function to New Delhi.[48]

Less regulation also meant that airlines would no longer need to demonstrate financial fitness in order to operate, nor would they need to have permission to reduce fares. Lower fares pioneered by the first European no-frills airline, the revitalised Ryanair, which abandoned all but five of its most profitable routes, placed considerable pressure on other airlines to reduce costs. The new entrant low-cost airlines operate on average at 43 per cent of the full-service airlines' operating costs. Airlines such as Ryanair and easyJet have not only entered but have flourished in the new aviation market with the latter airline among the most profitable in the UK in 2004. In 2002, Ryanair had a stock market valuation of £1.8 billion, some £30 million more than BA. In 2005 it became the largest international airline in Europe (by number of passengers carried). The success of the model encouraged BA to create its own low-cost subsidiary, Go, in 1999. Several other established UK airlines followed suit, launching low-cost subsidiaries including British Midland's bmibaby and the ill-fated MyTraveLite (MyTravel), while other airlines have offered low fares alongside their principal service; for example, charter airline Britannia Airlines launched BritanniaDirect.com. The impact of the low-cost airline on the full-service and charter sub-sector is reminiscent of the impact of the charter carriers on the short-haul full-service airlines in the 1960s, when the charter airlines 'infiltrated and diluted Europe's short haul market'.[49]

There are seven distinct components of low-cost airline operations which offer them a competitive advantage over the traditional scheduled operators:

1    The low-cost airlines fly at off-peak times from/to less congested airports where landing charges are lower and turnaround times are quicker. These airports are keen to attract scheduled traffic and attractive deals may be struck with regard to landing charges, ground staff, and baggage handling. Ryanair has pioneered this approach.
2    The low-cost airlines fly point-to-point, short routes, carrying passengers from one airport to another and returning to the airport of origin (hence, the low-cost airline has been likened to a bus company). As a result, the low-cost airline operates with higher crew utilisation and consequently lower crew costs.

3   The low-cost airlines provide a basic service. There is usually no in-flight catering although cabin crew onboard easyJet aircraft operate the easyKiosk, selling snacks and drinks.

4   The low-cost airlines operate at a higher seat density. In other words, leg room onboard is reduced in order to make more seats available per aircraft than on the same aircraft operated by their full-service competitors. They also achieve a higher load factor (i.e. number of passengers onboard each flight).

5   The low-cost airlines operate with minimum staff (e.g. the legal minimum of three cabin crew are employed on the Boeing 737),[50] who perform to high levels of productivity and efficiency. Ryanair carried 15 million passengers with only 2000 staff in 2002 compared to 35 million carried by BA with a staff of 55,000. ECA statistics show that whereas BA and bmi operate with 254 and 173 employees per aircraft respectively, Ryanair, Go, and easyJet operate with 36, 24, and 68 respectively.[51]

6   The low-cost airlines have until recently flown only one type of aircraft, the Boeing 737, because it is 'cheap, simple and ubiquitous'.[52] Southwest has operated with this aircraft for over 30 years to great effect.[53] Utilising a single type of aircraft saves on training costs, as flight and cabin crew need to be proficient in the operating systems of a single aircraft only.

7   The low-cost airlines operate independently of travel agencies, selling directly by phone or via the internet. This way, the airlines make cost savings by avoiding paying travel agency commission.

The crew cost savings are achieved by intensifying the crew workload, wich is made possible by the airline's point-to-point service that requires fewer overnight stays.[54] On average, low-cost airline pilot salaries are 27 per cent less than their full-service airline colleagues'. Despite this pay differential, low-cost airline pilots fly on average 210 days per annum, whereas full-service airline pilots fly on average only 184 days per annum.[55] Also, there is a much larger variable component of the low-cost airline pilot's salary. Sector pay is the term used to describe the variable component of the pilot's remuneration which is contingent on the number of flights (or sectors) the pilot flies. For low-cost airline pilots, variable sector pay represents a considerably larger proportion of their salary than it does for those pilots flying with full-service airlines. ECA statistics indicate that the average variable component of the salary of First Officers flying with full-service airlines is around 5 per cent. However, the same component for First Officers flying with low-cost airlines is around 18 per cent. The respective figures for Captains are 8 per cent and 20 per cent.[56]

The anticipated growth rate of the full-service airlines is dwarfed by the expected growth of the low-cost airlines, as demonstrated in Figure 2.1. This anticipated growth pattern has significant ramifications for pilots. The ECA estimate that the number of pilots required to meet demand for air transport will exceed 56,000 by 2010, compared with 38,000 employed in 2002. More than one in ten of these pilots will be employed by low-cost airlines, whereas only 4 per cent were employed in the same market sector in 2002. The ECA also anticipate that of the total demand for pilots in 2010, 30 per cent will be among the low-cost airlines, as illustrated in Figure 2.2.

As the representative voice of European pilots, the ECA are apprehensive about the growth of the low-cost sector as these airlines typically do not comply with the same 'community principles' to which the full-service operators adhere. In terms of labour, this involves 'fierce opposition' to the recognition of trade union representation within some low-cost airlines; failure to develop and respect labour (i.e. lack of training, job security, and quality of work life initiatives); and offering poor-quality jobs involving non-flying duties, compulsory relocation and pay for productivity.[57] In order to earn comparable salaries to their full-service airline counterparts, pilots at the low-cost airlines are expected to fly more frequent short sectors, and thus experience a more intense workload. Research into the safety implications of the workload of the low-cost airline pilot has shown that the low-cost model has led to 'excessive levels of stress and fatigue amongst flight crew'.[58]

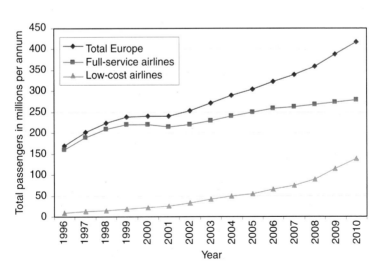

*Figure 2.1* Actual and anticipated growth rates of low-cost and full-service airlines compared (source: ECA 2002: 12).

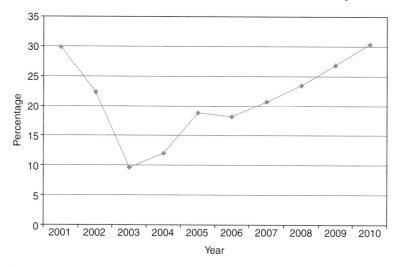

*Figure 2.2* Anticipated low-cost airline pilot recruitment as a percentage of total pilot recruitment (source: ECA 2002: 14).

Lower labour costs are fundamental to the low-cost airline model. However, the heightened competitive environment created by the success of the low-cost model means established airlines need to cut costs. As labour costs are an obvious target of such initiatives, management at established carriers have introduced a series of labour-focused cost reduction strategies. Principally, airlines have focused cost reduction strategies on reducing headcount.[59] For example, in a bid to be fit for privatisation, the UK's largest airline, BA, shed 37 per cent of its workforce between 1980 and 1984.[60] The threat of job losses has also been used to elicit diminished terms and conditions from the workforce. At Air2000, pilots agreed to a 5 per cent pay cut in order to save the jobs of 45 pilots. The airline had threatened to make 77 pilots redundant and demote a further 38 Captains to Co-pilot.

More flexible working practices have been introduced so that those employees remaining after a redundancy drive are able to cover the increased workload. In her study of UK cabin crew, Boyd finds evidence of 'draconian working conditions', as airlines extend working hours by manipulating shift patterns and eliminating rest breaks in order to maximise working time within legal duty hour limitations.[61] In tandem with the introduction of these practices, airlines have also frozen pay or managed to negotiate wage levels downwards.[62]

Other ways in which airlines have altered labour agreements have been by setting up low-cost subsidiaries or buying into or franchising smaller airlines. Employees' contracts within these subsidiaries have been inferior to those of staff employed by the parent airline. This policy is typified by BA and its franchisee airline City Flyer Express. Operating in BA livery, on BA domestic and regional routes out of Gatwick, City Flyer Express could achieve far lower unit costs than BA. BA launched its low-cost carrier Go with employee terms and conditions significantly lower than those of its mainline workforce.[63]

Outsourcing activities that were formerly performed in-house have also proved to be a popular cost reduction strategy.[64] By outsourcing activities, the airline allows market forces to drive down the costs of sub-contractors who tender for the business. For example, catering onboard BA flights is performed by Swissair's Gate Gourmet. Airlines have also used the threat of outsourcing to negotiate labour savings. The threat of outsourcing cargo handling allowed BA to reduce headcount within this department by 400 staff while obtaining a two-year pay freeze for the remaining employees.[65] Results of a survey of civil aviation unions affiliated to the International Transport Workers' Federation (ITF) into the effects of globalisation show that 50 per cent of participating unions reported that management had threatened to contract out core activities unless costs were reduced or efficiency improved.[66] The results of research into the impact of deregulation on employment relations in the airline industry reveal that the workforce has experienced job reductions, and where these have not occurred, management has enforced cost reductions to match the lowest-cost alternative supplier.[67]

## The new environment and the airline pilot

A survey of pilots' unions affiliated to the ECA explored the impact of the changes in the industry on the work experience of their members.[68] Whereas three-quarters of respondents perceived the effect of privatisation as positive, there was widespread concern about the outsourcing of work (69 per cent) and the impact of the low-cost airlines (54 per cent).[69] The effect of these forces on employment appears to be positive as the numbers of flight and cabin crew increased year on year for the five years prior to the study.[70] However, 15 per cent of respondents reported instances of compulsory redundancies in the five years prior to the survey.[71]

According to union officials, changes to work as a result of liberalisation and globalisation have had a negative impact on hours of work, management–labour relations, job satisfaction, work intensity, and health and safety, leading to more arduous flight deck jobs.[72] The unions were unanimous in reporting increases in working time over the previous five years, reflecting a variety of initiatives including increased frequency or duration of shifts, and reductions in rest periods and duty breaks.[73] In tandem with the intensification of flight deck jobs, a majority of respondents to the survey also claim either to have experienced the implementation of quality control initiatives or to be expecting such initiatives in the near future.[74] Thus, while flight deck jobs for European pilots were becoming more arduous, management were also expecting improvements in quality.

The globalisation of labour markets was also a concern for the respondents as 70 per cent of the European pilot unions' surveyed perceived global outsourcing to have impacted negatively on their members. One effect was the 'out-basing' of crews reported by 46 per cent of the respondents. A similar percentage reported the use of, or planned use of, 'wet leasing' arrangements. 'Wet lease' is the term used to describe the leasing of fully fuelled aircraft and crews who then don the leasing firm's uniform and livery, and fly its routes. Finally, 'benchmarking' strategies appeared to be prevalent among European airlines seeking cost reduction on various activities. By benchmarking against out-based or outsourced activities, management has been able to establish lower market rates for certain routes. Two-thirds of respondents reported benchmarking within airlines employing their members while 54 per cent of respondents claimed that management had used the threat of outsourcing to reduce costs.[75]

It is clear that airline pilots have not been exempt from the negative effects of restructuring within airlines as a result of increased competition. However, UK pilots have not passively succumbed to the negative effects of these industry developments, as demonstrated by the threat of strike action at BA in 1996. In order to avert the action, management were forced to rethink elements of the Business Efficiency Programme (BEP), proposed by the then chief executive, Robert Ayling. Whereas flight crew have, on occasion, been able to resist changes that are deemed unacceptable by the majority, the ramifications of 9/11 for the civil aviation industry have resulted in irresistible changes to both work benefits and conditions.

## September 11

The events of September 11 2001 are well documented. The effect of these tragic events on the civil aviation industry has been profound. The Chairperson of the ILO Think Tank on the Impact of the 11 September Events for Civil Aviation (Geneva, 29–30 October 2001) described the terrorist attacks as:

> unlike any other shock experienced by the industry to date. They have had a unique, unprecedented, devastating and immediate impact on all segments of the industry (airlines, air navigation service providers,

airports, maintenance and catering providers, etc.) with unpredictable economic and social consequences.[76]

Prior to September 2001, the global civil aviation industry was already entering a 'trough'. Data for world air traffic in the period immediately preceding the terrorist attacks on New York showed that both passenger traffic and air freight were already experiencing a downturn in demand (see Figure 2.3). In the days before the attacks, BA's chief executive officer Rod Eddington claimed that the airline would have to reduce labour expenses through 1800 job losses, due to a decline in premium passenger traffic over the year 2001. Nonetheless, the impact of 9/11 on the industry, and in particular the workers (flight and cabin crew) whose place of work (the aircraft) had been used as a weapon, was quite simply profound. Figure 2.3 illustrates the dramatic fall in traffic, expressed in terms of revenue passenger kilometre (RPK) and revenue tonne kilometre (RTK).

The reduction in traffic for the year 2001 represented the largest annual fall ever recorded in the industry. Those airlines hardest hit in the UK and Ireland were those dependent on transatlantic traffic. BA recorded its biggest losses (£200 million) since privatisation in 1987, while Virgin Atlantic also faced substantial losses (£94 million). In October 2001, job losses announced at bmi, Britannia, and KLM amounted to 3400.[77] In November 2001, the charter airlines Air2000 and JMC both announced extensive cutbacks. Air2000 announced 400 redundancies and closed its base at Newcastle airport, while JMC closed three of its regional bases.[78]

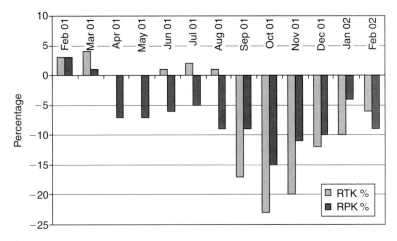

*Figure 2.3* World air traffic, 2001–2002.

A report commissioned by the International Labour Organisation illustrates the extent of numerical and financial flexibility measures for civil aviation employees introduced by management among the world's airlines in response to the crisis.[79] In the UK, management opted to reduce headcount and/or employee remuneration immediately, and engage in post hoc negotiation with unions and labour representatives, exacerbating the worsening state of the employment relationship.

The impact of these events was felt not only in terms of financial and numerical cuts, but also in terms of the organisation of work. For pilots, changes to the cockpit were introduced because of the way in which the terrorists were able to gain control of the aircraft. Principally, the introduction of the locked flight deck door adopted by many airlines proved deeply unpopular among the flight crew community as it reduced communication between flight and cabin crews and undermined the authority of the Captain on board.

## Summary

The management of people in the civil aviation industry is complicated by the pro-cyclical nature of the industry and the proportion and malleability of labour costs. These factors have combined to necessitate cost cutting and to ensure that those cuts are often focused on the labour. Liberalisation and intensified globalisation have presented management with both the motive and the opportunity to reduce costs.[80] However, management prerogative is not absolute as industrial action on the part of employees can be extremely costly due to the perishable nature of the product. Indeed, industrial action was an important determinant in the demise of the crisis-struck Belgian airline, Sabena. It is clear then that the competent management of people in airlines is extremely important.

This importance is heightened in the management of flight crew who through voice or exit can impose severe sanctions on the airline. Pilots occupy a position of considerable bargaining power and have not been averse to exercising that power. Flight crew are also an extremely valuable commodity for airlines due to their extensive training and their scarcity. It is imperative, then, that management generate a committed and satisfied flight crew community. To that end, HRM promises a great deal to airline management. The following chapter provides an overview of arguably the most prominent people management strategy in the last 20 years, HRM.

# 3 The content and style of human resource management

## Introduction

Human resource management (HRM) has for some time been the dominant theme in people management and employee relations research, despite much debate about what it is.[1] In *Reassessing Human Resource Management* (1992), Blyton and Turnbull refer to the 'central uncertainty' of HRM, noting that the 'ways in which the term is used by academics and practitioners indicates both variations in meaning and significantly different emphases on what constitute its core components'.[2] This ambiguity has persisted some 15 years after the publication of Blyton and Turnbull's text.

In general, advocates agree that HRM involves managing people to achieve mutual advantage for management and employee. But how is this achieved and what constitutes HRM? Throughout the 1980s and 1990s and even in contemporary accounts, attention has been focused on the policies and practices associated with HRM, referred to as the *content* of HRM in this book. HR policies and practices play a central role in each of the models purporting to explain the effect of HRM. In the Michigan model[3] of HRM, policies concerning selection, appraisal, reward, and development are fundamental, whereas the Harvard model[4] foregrounds the crucial importance of employee influence, rewards systems, and work organisation. Although contingent upon the operating strategy of the firm, HR policy and practice in planning, selection, appraisal, remuneration, and training remain central to the Rutgers model.[5] The Warwick model[6] takes an open systems view of the firm and states that the HR policies and practices (in planning, work organisation, reward and employee relations) are influenced by both the internal and the external organisational environments. Finally, the Bath model[7] concentrates on the competent implementation process of policy and practice in the success of HRM, adopting the label 'organizational process advantage'[8] from Boxall.[9] However, this model also emphasises 11 policy areas of importance.

Content has featured extensively in studies of HRM. For example, in his widely cited study of over 900 US firms, Huselid[10] reports a substantial return on investment in 'high performance work practices' in terms of lower labour turnover and higher profitability. In the UK, Patterson and his colleagues find similar results when investigating the impact of people management practices.[11] Patrick Wright and his colleagues at the Center for Advanced Human Resource Studies at Cornell University have previously explained the way in which HRM benefits firm performance explicitly in terms of the content of HRM. Their proposition draws on the resource-based theory (RBT) of the firm, pioneered by Penrose[12] and adopted by Barney[13] for application in this context, which views the firm as 'a collection of productive resources'.[14] These are defined as the human, physical, and organisational resources,[15] each of which, if rare, valuable, inimitable, and non-substitutable,[16] offer the firm a sustained competitive advantage. For Wright and his colleagues the knowledge, skills, and abilities (KSA) of the people in the firm (the human resource) are rare, inimitable, and non-substitutable, but not inherently a source of value.[17] Not only do HR practices enhance the KSA of the employees, they also motivate employees to utilise their faculties to the optimum level. Hence, the keys to unlocking the potential of employee KSA are HR practices:

> although HR practices are not themselves sources of sustained competitive advantage, they play an important role in developing sustained competitive advantage through the development of the human capital pool, and through moderating the relationship between this pool and sustained competitive advantage by affecting HR behaviour.[18]

For Wright and his colleagues, HRM policies and practices impact on employee attitudes, which are subsequently reflected in the employees' behaviour. The authors of the Bath model of HRM adopt a similar perspective, but rely on the AMO rubric of performance (discussed below) to explain the impact of HRM. Purcell and his colleagues discern 11 HRM policy areas including sophisticated recruitment and selection, training and development, performance appraisal, and job security, along with team working, career opportunity, communication, involvement, pay satisfaction, job challenge, and work–life balance. However, *process* is critical in the Bath model, which emphasises the role of the line manager in 'implementing, enacting, leading and controlling',[19] thereby encouraging an environment of trust and respect in order to bring such policies to life. With successful implementation of these policies the firm stands to enhance the ability of employees to do the job (the A of AMO) and to present them with the opportunity to demonstrate discretionary effort (the

O of AMO). The policies and practices also increase the motivation of the employee (the M of AMO), driving them to use their improved ability through incentives. In their recent bestseller, *Freakonomics*,[20] Levitt and Dubner remind us of the three forms of positive incentive. These are economic incentives, social incentives, and moral incentives. HRM promises to provide all three. Economic incentives are present in schemes of remuneration linked to performance such as performance-related pay. Social incentives are generated through practices such as team working (although the critical appraisal of team working by Parker and Slaughter, for example,[21] would suggest otherwise). Finally, a moral incentive results from an obligation on the part of the employee to reciprocate the organisational support shown by management expressed in reorganising work to the benefit of the employee, which is central to the social exchange theory of HRM.[22]

There has been considerable concern for the fate of trade unions under HRM. The threat from HRM to trade unions can be broadly categorised as the increasing individualisation of the employment contract and the generation of organisational commitment.[23] With regard to the former, trade unions generally negotiated common wage rates for the collective so that employment contracts were equitable. However, HRM policies and practices like performance-related pay 'undermine the *raison d'etre* of unions: bargaining the effort-wage contract'.[24] These policies appeal to instrumental, rational-economic motives and diminish the solidarity of employees, leading to an individual, rather than a collective, orientation. Legge opines that if indeed organisations treat their employees as their most valuable asset then the need for trade union protection against 'arbitrary and exploitative management is reduced and the role of existing unions is thereby diminished and unions marginalised'.[25] As for the latter factor, organisational commitment, a central aim of HRM is to elicit this response from employees. Policies and practices such as sophisticated processes of recruitment, induction, and training are used in order to socialise employees, thereby encouraging them to accept the norms and goals of the firm as their own. An argument within this debate holds that commitment to the organisation necessarily diminishes commitment to the union (this is discussed further in Chapter 7). Research by Hoell buttresses this thesis as he finds that organisational commitment and commitment to the union are inversely related.[26] This raised the question of whether HRM is a deliberate anti-union strategy.

For Kelly, HRM and industrial relations are independent, antithetical management strategies.[27] He argues that since the late 1970s trade unionism has faced 'a dramatic and far-reaching employer and state offensive',[28] with employers expressing militancy towards trade unions in four ways:

'hostility to union recognition, de-recognition, antipathy to collective bargaining and attempts to bypass and marginalise workplace trade unionism'.[29] Kelly reasons that HRM is inherently incompatible with trade unionism because the effect of the former necessarily diminishes the influence of the latter. Kelly cites the prevalence of high commitment management (HCM) practices in unionised workplaces as evidence of an employer strategy to rid the workplace of unionism.[30] He writes,

> if human resource management is in some sense anti-union it *would* be most common in the unionised sector because that is where employers have most need of its anti-union effects. By contrast, since most non-union employers face no immediate prospect of unionization then there is little sign of human resource management in that sector.[31]

Guest[32] acknowledges the possible threat to trade unions posed by HRM owing to its central aim of eliciting enhanced organisational commitment precisely because 'a worker who is committed to the organization is unlikely to become involved "industrial relations" or any type of collective activity'.[33] In other words, the highly committed worker is less likely to feel the need, or even desire, for union affiliation. However, Guest states that it is possible for the firm to pursue both high industrial relations activity and concomitantly high HRM activity. Citing evidence of the coexistence of HRM and traditional industrial relations within firms,[34] he argues that HRM and trade unions are not mutually exclusive and can indeed coexist in the New Realism[35] of the workplace. For Guest, partnership is a sustainable condition wherein trade unions exist in an environment of high HRM activity.[36] Guest clearly understands HRM and industrial relations as distinct though compatible.

More recently, Boxall and Purcell have revitalised the eclectic interpretation of HRM, which has an established tradition in the UK and which presents HRM as indistinguishable from employment relations.[37] In contrast to Guest and Kelly, they contend that industrial relations activity is encapsulated in HRM which represents the totality of people management activity, i.e. all aspects of the management of the human resource. They suggest that HRM is neither inherently compatible with, nor antithetical to, industrial relations; what counts is the degree of collectivism in HRM.[38] Drawing on Purcell's[39] earlier concept of management style, the authors distinguish an alternative component to the commonly featured HRM content. The more common surface layer of policies and practices (HRM content) which has featured in much of the HRM research is accompanied by an underpinning layer of process and philosophy, which encompasses the dimensions of individualism and

collectivism. Following this analytical distinction, this book differenti-
ates the policies and practices implemented in the workplace, or content
of HRM, from the HRM style.

## HRM style

Drawing largely on management style, HRM style refers to the choices
made and the underlying rationale for the way in which management treats
its employees. It implies a 'distinctive set of guiding principles, written or
otherwise, which set parameters to and signposts for management action
in the way employees are treated and particular events handled'.[40] Individualism refers to the 'extent to which the firm gives credence to the feelings
and sentiments of each employee and seeks to develop and encourage each
employee's capacity and role at work'.[41] The degree of individualism in
HRM style is apparent in the way in which management behave towards
the individual employee. It differs from individualism in management
style in one very important way. Purcell's notion of individualism in management style appears to be synonymous with HRM content. For example,
Purcell notes that commitment to individualism might be expressed by

> strong features of internal labour markets with careful selection at
> restricted points of entry, internal training schemes, promotion ladders
> and extensive welfare provisions, including relatively high pay.
> Payment systems might emphasize merit elements and make use of
> appraisal and assessment techniques designed to distinguish the contri-
> bution of each employee in anything from 'attitudes to attributes' ... .
> Attitude surveys may well be used regularly since such organizations
> are keen to assess the efficacy of their policies. Communication
> systems are likely to be extensive and developed through a variety of
> media from newspapers and videos to personal contact between the
> manager, the individual and small groups of employees'.[42]

However, HRM policies and practices are no reliable indication of the
degree of credence offered to the feelings and sentiments of employees.
For example, such policies and practices may have been implemented by
management in response to mimetic pressure to conform with the HRM
strategy of a successful competitor, or in order to encourage employees to
remain with the firm because a tight external labour market constrains the
possibility of recruiting to replace disgruntled employees. Conversely, a
firm might respect the feelings and sentiments of employees without
having the capital to invest in such sophisticated policies and practices.
Individualism in HRM style is not reducible to such readily observable

management initiatives. Rather, it denotes the more general attitude of management towards, and treatment of, employees.

Purcell charts individualism in management style along a continuum between people having a commodity status (low individualism) and people having a resource status (high individualism), identifying three degrees along the way (labour control, paternalism, and employee development). Whereas Purcell charts the *degree* to which the firm gives credence to the feelings and sentiments of each employee and seeks to develop and encourage each employee's capacity and role, a more rudimentary assessment was made of HRM style at the airlines in this study. The measures of individualism in HRM style are discussed further in Chapter 5.

Like its precedent in the management style framework, collectivism in HRM style is defined as 'the extent to which the organization recognizes the rights of employees to have a say in those aspects of management decision making which concerns them'.[43] Collectivism concerns the extent to which management recognise the collective interests of employees, their collective involvement in the decision-making processes and the legitimacy accorded the collective by management. Purcell notes that high, or cooperative, collectivism in management style can be expressed in non-union firms, in the legitimacy afforded by management to such representative mechanisms as works councils.[44] The essence of collectivism is the 'approach of management in operating these joint structures. Do they seek to minimise or oppose them or actively co-operate with them?'[45] This is crucial because, alone, recognition of trade unions or the existence of a works council, for example, may offer a false indication of the collectivism in HRM style, as noted by Purcell:

> In many cases unions have fought to be recognised against management's wishes and labour law is important in some countries in imposing requirements on firms to deal with work councils or recognise trade unions. Given the existence of collective employee organizations, management can however choose the extent to which they legitimise, de facto, the collective and joint structures of negotiation and consultation.[46]

Purcell plots collectivism in management style along the continuum from unitarism, where unions are actively resisted, through adversarialism, towards cooperation.[47] The latter refers to the situation in which, to quote Purcell again, 'an attempt is made to build constructive relationships with employee organizations and incorporate them into the organizational fabric. Broad ranging discussions are held with extensive information provided on a whole range of decisions and plans including aspects of strategic management'.[48] It is important, he notes, to distinguish this style from the adversarial or constitutional collectivist style whereby unions are recognised, but wherein 'management control is emphasized with the aim of minimising or neutralizing union constraints on both operational and strategic management'.[49] Therefore, a high degree of collectivism requires not just union recognition, but genuine meaningful union engagement in matters of strategic and operational importance. As the Employment Relations Act (1999) has been generally effective in ensuring union recognition in workplaces where the majority of employees desire third party representation, a unitarist approach is unlikely where union representation is widely desirable. Once again, it is important to differentiate collectivism in management style from collectivism in HRM style. A high degree of collectivism in management style can be expressed where collective representation does not necessarily involve an independent third party but goes through an in-house works council system. A high degree of collectivism in HRM style must be expressed through a genuine or meaningful engagement with a trade union. This is discussed further in Chapter 5. The categories of collectivism in HRM style in this study are those of adversarial and cooperative.

To be sure, HRM may be understood in terms of content (HRM policies and practices implemented in the management of people), and in terms of style (the way in which management approach employment relations). HRM content does not explicitly define a role for trade unions, but inevitably has an impact on trade unions. It is the HRM style that reflects managerial intention for the HRM content. HRM policies and practices such as performance-related pay, which individualises the employment relationship 'because it isolates employees and personalises issues such as design and evaluation of work',[50] is not incompatible with a highly collective HRM style. For example, at Southwest Airlines, where this practice coexists with high union density (around 80 per cent) and cooperative collectivism in its HRM style.[51]

## HRM and employee attitudes

This analytical distinction between content and style might prove invaluable in explaining the disparity in findings of research into the impact of HRM, especially on the attitudes of employees. Employee attitudes may be a more reliable measure of the impact of HRM, given the complex dynamic of firm performance that is glossed over by much research in this field, leading to critical reviews by commentators in both the UK and the US.[52] A common criticism centres on the complexity of firm performance which ensures that *any* link between HRM and firm performance is neither explained nor explicitly proved, and is therefore causally ambiguous.

Purcell,[53] for example, argues that much of the HRM research carried out in the 1990s ignores the complex interplay of the firm's context and the implementation of HRM. He duly notes that research which merely measures the existence of HRM policies and practices fails to explore the context and the manner in which the practice was introduced. Legge[54] also acknowledges the convoluted interplay of multifarious variables which makes any assessment of the impact of HRM on firm performance extremely difficult, if not impossible. The author suggests a refocus of the debate on employee outcomes such as job satisfaction and involvement in the decision-making processes of the firm.

Delaney and Godard present a similar critique. They raise the problem of the 'missing variable', referring to any extraneous variable which has not been identified in the researcher's model, but which may be responsible for the fluctuation in a firm's performance. Hence, undue significance may have been attributed to the effect of HRM.[55] Godard[56] argues that ailing firms may implement what he terms alternative work practices (AWP) in order to improve performance. Therefore, measurement may conflate previous poor performance with the impact of AWP. Conversely, successful firms may be able to invest in sophisticated HRM, whereas less profitable or successful firms are not able to invest in this luxury. Hence, not only is the HRM/firm performance link causally ambiguous, but in many cases causality may run from performance to HRM rather than from HRM to performance.

The problem of causality in the relationship between HRM and firm performance renders research of this nature unreliable. Legge[57] considers this approach no more than a 'spent round'. Consequently, a revised research agenda[58] has been proposed, which calls for a refocusing of research to evaluate the impact of HRM on the attitudes of the employee. Employee attitudes might also be influenced by other factors, but the nexus between HRM and employee attitudes is far less convoluted. Whereas firm performance might be the result of various extraneous variables, the link between HRM and employee attitudes is less tenuous as HRM impacts directly on the employee who is a participant in, and consumer of, HRM. Indeed, members of the Center for Advanced Human Resource Studies at Cornell University have argued that measuring employee attitudes is the *most* appropriate indicator of the impact of HRM, because HRM '*can only impact firm performance through the behaviour and attitude of employees*'.[59]

Two commonly cited attitudinal indicators of the impact of HRM are job satisfaction and organisational commitment.[60] Both feature as outcomes of HRM in the recent Bath model where they are considered to be important determinants of discretionary effort, which is in turn believed to be the way in which the firm is able to gain a competitive advantage through its workforce. There is wider support for this thesis. Research has shown that job attitudes, particularly job satisfaction and organisational commitment, are significant predictors of employee performance, lower absence, lower 'tardiness', and reduced turnover.[61]

Prior research specifically aimed at measuring attitudinal response to HRM has produced mixed findings. Of the UK studies, Guest has found positive response on the part of employees within firms where HRM policies and practices have been introduced. In his study commissioned by the Chartered Institute of Personnel and Development (CIPD), contingent pay and internal promotion were associated with motivation, whereas team working and autonomy led to enhanced involvement and participation.[62] Ramsay and his colleagues[63] tested the impact of HR policies and practices emphasising high commitment and high involvement on the attitudes of employees using data from the 1998 Workplace Employee Relations Survey (WERS98). On the basis of the WERS98 data, the authors were unable to find support for either of the models. While the longitudinal study carried out by Truss and her colleagues at the Bristol site of Hewlett Packard reveals commitment to best practice HRM and sound financial performance. However, employees at the firm were experiencing low morale and high stress.[64]

Error in measurement has been cited as a possible explanation of the disparity in findings of HRM research. Measurement of HRM content has drawn considerable criticism. Wright and his colleagues have criticised previous research for failing to measure HRM content accurately. They highlight significant random error in studies dependent on single respondent data. Consequently, they conclude that 'individual raters, even highly knowledgeable job incumbents, provide highly unreliable information about HR practices'.[65] Wright and Boswell distinguish between the firm's HR policies, which represent the stated intention of the firm with regard to HRM, and the actual HR practices it has implemented. The authors use this distinction to critique previous HRM research and state that there has been no small amount of ambiguity concerning what has been tested by researchers who have relied upon single management respondent data: have they tested the impact of actual practices or intended policies?[66] Incidentally, in order to resolve this issue, airline pilots rather than HR management were asked to identify the practices used at their airlines in the management of flight crew in this study.

## The effect of content and style

Measurement issues aside, moderating variables have become fashionable in explanations of the way in which HRM works. For Meyer and Smith,[67] the success of HRM policies and practices is predicated upon employee interpretation. They have argued that the efficacy of HRM content is contingent on the way in which the employee perceives managerial rationale in implementing such policies and practices. They note:

> employees' commitment to their organization was related to their belief that the organization's HRM practices were motivated by a desire to attract and retain good employees. In contrast, commitment was unrelated to perceptions that HRM practices were motivated by a desire to increase productivity or to comply with employment laws. In light of these findings, it cannot be assumed that the implementation of a particular practice (e.g. training) will necessarily enhance commitment. Rather, the implementation of training might induce employees to consider the organization's motivation; whether commitment is influenced or not might depend, in turn, on the results of this attributional analysis.[68]

For HRM content to be successful, then, employees must be convinced of benign managerial intent. By contrast, a widespread perception of managerial cynicism and pragmatism is likely to be detrimental to the effectiveness of HRM policies and practices. In such circumstances, HRM content is likely either to have little impact or to have a negative impact on employee attitudes and behaviours as employees read them as work intensification.[69] In their own analysis Meyer and Smith find that employee perception of organisational support mediates the impact of HRM policies and practices.

Perceived organisational support[70] is a concept familiar to social exchange theorists, who claim that a relationship develops between employee and organisation in the same way that a relationship develops between two people. Actions by parties engaged in this social exchange are based on experience of prior exchanges in the relationship, and governed by the norm of reciprocity. In the organisational setting, where the firm demonstrates commitment to the employee, the employee is likely to respond in kind out of a sense of obligation to reciprocate the behaviour. Where the firm offers organisational support to the employee, the employee is more likely to demonstrate organisational commitment in return.[71] The definition of organisational support developed by Eisenberger and his colleagues, and described as the extent to which the organisation values the contribution of employees and cares about their well-being,[72] resonates with the notion of individualism in HRM style. Both identify the importance of a deeper commitment from the organisation to the employee, beyond the surface or content layer of HRM.[73] Therefore, individualism in

HRM style might be an important factor in the success of HRM policies and practices.

The argument holds that HRM policies and practices are more likely to have a positive impact where the employee perceives organisational support and is convinced of benign managerial intent. Benign intent and organisational support are expressed through both individualism *and* collectivism in HRM style. With regard to the latter, Guest has argued that the coexistence of trade unions with HRM provides employees with a 'safeguard or safety net',[74] which goes some way to assuaging the anxiety resulting from changes in the work environment caused by HRM. Union presence might serve to assuage employee anxiety of unchallenged managerial prerogative and guarantee against the imposition of unacceptable workplace reform, thereby encouraging employees to 'buy in' to new policies and practices. Collectivism in HRM style, i.e. the extent to which the union is genuinely engaged by management, is liable to have a positive association with the degree to which employees buy in to HRM policies and practices. We know that HRM policies and practices are more likely to be found in unionised workplaces[75] and the WERS98 team claim that workplaces with a recognised union and extensive HRM policies and practices 'did better than average, and better than workplaces without recognition and a minority of these practices'.[76] There is prima facie evidence that HRM style moderates the impact of HRM content on the attitudes of employees.

## Convergence on HRM content and style

This chapter has distinguished two dimensions of HRM. First, HRM content refers to the workplace-level policies and practices implemented in the management of employees. Second, HRM style reflects the way in which management treat labour, individually and collectively. As the analysis includes data from airlines operating in a diverse range of market sub-sectors, a second aim of the study was to assess the level of convergence either on models of HRM specific to the market sub-sector, in line with best external fit[77] logic, or on a model of best practice HRM[78] across the market sub-sectors. Convergence on HRM content was assessed by measuring the use of specific policies and practices in the management of airline pilots. Convergence on HRM style was assessed by examining airline treatment of pilots and by exploring the relationship between airline management and BALPA.

The question of convergence on HRM is an issue of resurgent interest in the field.[79] DiMaggio and Powell[80] identify three forces for convergence, which are intensified in complex[81] and dynamic[82] environments.

The civil aviation environment is complex and dynamic, wherein competent people management is critical and mistakes are costly. As the previous chapter has shown, managing pilots competently is a fundamental requirement for any airline as the cost of getting it wrong can be severe. In such an environment the potential for isomorphism in management practice is greatly enhanced.

Central to the theory of institutional isomorphism is the assertion that individual efforts to deal rationally with uncertainty and constraint often lead to homogeneity.[83] Hence, disparate organisations in the same line of business are subject to powerful forces which lead them to become increasingly similar. DiMaggio and Powell identify three pressures towards isomorphism. First, coercion exerted by government legislation and dominant organisations forces institutions to operate in similar ways (coercive isomorphism). Second, uncertainty generated by the environment leads to imitation, whereby organisations model themselves on other (successful) organisations (mimetic isomorphism). The process of modelling may be either intentional or unintentional. Intentional modelling may occur through the diffusion of best practice via consultants or trade associations or via sophisticated resourcing such as 'headhunting'. In a similar vein, unintentional modelling may occur through the transfer of staff, new recruits bringing concepts from their previous workplace into the organisation. Third, normative isomorphism is the result of the professionalisation of the workforce, whereby professional workers adhere to a code of conduct external to the organisation. The increased professionalisation of the workforce ensures that operating procedures of professionals are standardised across organisations.

Within the UK airline industry, all three of these pressures are evident. The first, coercive isomorphism, is exercised through government legislation and through the ubiquitous regulations set by the Civil Aviation Authority (CAA). Regardless of geographical region or operational context, each airline must operate to strict industry guidelines. Mimetic isomorphism has increased as the airline industry has been liberalised. There has been some debate about whether this has led to a convergence of management practice in the industry,[84] but within market sub-sectors there now appear to be prevailing formulas for success (e.g. the low cost or no-frills model developed by Southwest Airlines has been widely imitated). In some cases, traditional full-service airlines have transformed themselves wholesale into low-cost outfits, as in the case of British European, which in 2002 transformed its traditional scheduled operation to the low-cost model and was renamed FlyBE. The success of the low-cost model has caused an isomorphism in the full-service sector as traditional scheduled airlines have placed greater emphasis on the quality of service they provide while trying to minimise costs and reduce their tariffs. Finally, normative isomorphism is a feature of the work of flight crew who, despite developing airline-specific skills and knowledge, must first undergo extensive generic training and must pass generic industry evaluations every six months in order to retain their licence. Like other professional groups, pilots adhere to strict professional guidelines in their work.

Evidently there is considerable pressure for airline management to converge on a similar HRM strategy, especially in the management of pilots. However, a recent analysis of the US airline industry by Gittell and her colleagues finds that there remains considerable difference in the collectivism in HRM style of major carriers.[85] The first of three distinct approaches to industrial relations is the union avoidance policy pursued by Delta and by Continental Airlines under Frank Lorenzo,[86] although in recent times the strategy at Continental has changed dramatically. At Delta, management adopted a paternalistic approach in order to substitute unions, 'offering high wages, lifetime employment and a "family" culture'.[87] Under Lorenzo, Continental Airlines suppressed union influence and withdrew recognition of the pilots' and mechanics' unions. The second strategy, pursued by United, Northwest, Eastern, and Western Airlines, is categorised as shared governance.[88] The most consistent shared governance policy has been pursued by United Airlines, where an extensive Employee Stock Ownership Plan (ESOP) has been in place since 1994. Finally, there is the high-trust workplace culture evident in the management–labour relationship at Southwest Airlines and the 'new' Continental Airlines. This diversity in HRM style demonstrates the level of strategic choice[89] airline management is able to impose despite the forces for convergence. It is interesting, therefore, to assess the level of convergence among UK airlines in terms of both HRM content and HRM style.

## HRM and trade unions

The final objective of the study was to examine the implications of HRM for trade unions. It is overly simplistic to conclude that cooperative collectivism is an unmitigated 'good' for trade unions, whereas adversarial collectivism is bad. For example, whereas cooperative collectivism might provide the union with an established position in the firm, it might also lead to a widespread feeling among members that the union is no longer able to represent their interests independently. Consequently, union membership might decline. Alternatively, adversarial collectivism might mean that the union is not integrated into the decision-making machinery of the firm, but such managerial resistance might result in a resurgence of traditional trade unionism. Hence, it is argued that the implications of HRM for trade unions very much depend upon the attitudes of members towards their trade union and an imperative thus exists for such data.

Trade union cooperation has become prominent in recent years as a result of the New Labour government's promotion of 'partnership' and the new statutory recognition procedure embodied in the Employment Relations Act (1999). Efforts to engage trade unions are very much a recent development, following many years of marginalisation. The individualisation of the workforce throughout the 1980s and 1990s has been variously attributed to changes in labour law, and the emergence of new work practices associated with HRM. Guest defines the former in terms of the Conservative governments' persistent 'creeping attack on the unions through successive legislation'.[90] Changes in legislation undermining collectivism include the abolition of the 'closed shop' and extensive restrictions on legitimate industrial action.[91] HRM policies and practices such as performance-related pay and direct communication enable management to bypass the trade unions, communicating and negotiating directly with the employee. With a large part of its traditional purpose usurped, the future for trade unions appeared to be bleak. Membership density declined from 56 per cent in 1979 to 30 per cent in 1998 although since then it has stabilised.[92]

The success of New Labour at the General Election in 1997 brought with it the notion of social partnership, 'the institutional process of applying the spirit of business ethics and theory of stake-holding to the employment relationship'.[93] The Involvement and Participation Association (IPA) set out the following criteria for a genuine partnership agreement:

- joint commitment to the success of the enterprise;
- mutual recognition of each party's legitimate interests and a commitment to resolve differences in an atmosphere of trust;
- a commitment to employment security;
- a focus on the quality of work life;
- transparency and sharing of information; and
- mutual gains for both unions and employers, delivering concrete improvements to business performance, employee involvement, and terms and conditions.

Prima facie, social partnership offers trade unions a more active role in the firm than was available during the 'Ten Lean Years' of Conservative suppression.[94] Consequently, the Trades Union Congress (TUC) readily advocated social partnership. Whereas the rationale for trade unions to buy into the idea appeared self-evident, the business case for doing so is more convoluted.

Ackers and Payne explain the managerial interest in social partnership in terms of the relative failure of attempts to bypass the trade unions and incorporate employees more fully in the business. Implicit in this explanation is managerial awareness of the moderating effect that collectivism in HRM style has in encouraging employees to buy in to HRM. Rather than marginalising the role of the trade union, a policy that was met with suspicion and often resulted in opposition to new work practices, trade unions were incorporated so that they could legitimise new work practices; 'as a result some employers now court union support to make [employee involvement] work'.[95] Ackers and Payne contrast two outcomes of social partnership for trade unions. First, they criticise the argument that partnership is a unitarist 'ploy' to 'further compromise the independence of unions from management and quicken their decline'.[96] Social partnership, in this reading, demands the demobilisation of membership, rendering it vulnerable to management prerogative. In contrast, they support a second and considerably more optimistic view of social partnership as a 'revamped version of pluralism that sustained union influence',[97] by focusing on the opportunity it offers for trade unions to re-enter the 'mainstream of political and industrial life'.[98] Through compromise and accommodation, the trade union displays itself as a responsible stakeholder. Once a foothold is regained in political and industrial life, the trade union is able to regulate management decision- and strategy-making based on the interests of its members.

If we move from theory to practice, the study of 11 public and private sector partnership firms conducted by Oxenbridge and Brown distinguishes two faces of partnership. Firms within their sample have introduced partnership for one of two purposes: in order either to *nurture* or to *contain* collective bargaining.[99] Unions engaged in partnerships of the nurturing type were rewarded with more frequent involvement with management and regained a proactive role in employment regulation.[100] However, this appears to be the full extent to which unions have benefited, because, as the authors point out, 'This did not prevent management in some firms seeking greater control over communication structures, and trying to shift worker loyalty away from the union'.[101]

Advocacy of social partnership has met with vehement opposition from critics. Kelly, for example, takes exception to what he perceives as trade union capitulation required by partnership. He cites research findings that confirm 'a generally more aggressive stance towards unions' to argue that HRM is inherently anti-union.[102] Kelly argues that by adopting a moderate, collaborative approach to management, trade unions legitimise the new work practices of HRM and will, therefore, inevitably be complicit in accelerating their own demise. This perspective is bolstered by evidence of managerial cynicism and pragmatism in implementing partnerships. Findings of the study carried out by Bacon and Storey[103] show that unions were invited to sign post hoc partnership agreements in order to legitimise substantial changes in work organisation already unilaterally determined by management. In discussion of their findings the authors state that although

> the new agreements did in the main re-establish a role for trade unions and offered forums to establish joint rules and procedures … the agreements were firmly management-driven … [and] a significant proportion would clearly have been happier with continued progress towards union exclusion.[104]

The impact of partnership, positive or negative, on the trade union will be expedited by the perception of its efficacy by the union membership. If, on the one hand, members perceive adequate, or better, representation by the union, then the future of the union may be assured. On the other hand, should they feel that the union is too weak to effectively represent their interests or to make a difference, rank-and-file members might withdraw their membership, potentially resulting in the demise of trade unionism in the workplace.

It is clear that whereas cooperative collectivism reflects a less threatening stance on the part of management towards trade unions, the union decision of whether to engage in partnership should be heavily dependent on the wishes of the membership. It is thus extremely important to assess the extent of pilots' desire for a cooperative relationship typified by partnership between their union and airline management, as this may be critical to the success of BALPA.

## Summary

The intention was for this chapter to set the theoretical scene for the analysis in subsequent chapters. It has distinguished HRM content from HRM style and justified an investigation of the incidence of both components and the impact of each on the attitudes of pilots in the UK airline industry. Collectivism in HRM style is intrinsically linked to industrial relations activity and trade unions. The chapter also confirms the necessity for an evaluation of pilots' attitudes towards cooperation between union and management, expressed in a partnership agreement. The following chapter describes the research project, data collection methods and techniques of data analysis.

# 4 The research project

## A methodology

## Introduction

The study on which this book is based was carried out over a four-year period, between 2001 and 2005, and was sponsored by an Economic and Social Research Council grant. The study collected and analysed qualitative and quantitative data. This chapter discusses the methods of data collection and data analysis. The original study sourced data from BALPA officials and representatives, airline management and pilots at 24 airlines. For convenience of analysis, six airlines were selected from the three main market sub-sectors in the UK civil aviation industry. In order to compare airlines of the same market sub-sector, two airlines were selected from each. The full-service airlines, BA and bmi, were selected, along with two low-cost airlines, easyJet and Go, and two charter airlines, Britannia[1] and Air2000.[2] The research has utilised essentially four methods of data collection: secondary data collection, interviews, focus groups, and a large-scale questionnaire survey.

## Secondary data analysis

Background information concerning the airlines comprising the sample was drawn from secondary sources. The style of HRM at the six sample airlines, reported in Chapter 5, is largely based on secondary source data. A disadvantage of such data is that they can be inappropriate and incomplete.[3] Whereas easyJet and BA have been the focus of several previous studies,[4] and Barbara Cassani published a book in December 2003 on tenure as CEO of Go,[5] very little has been written of pilot management in the charter airlines. The secondary data sources used include prior airline research, company reports, newspaper articles, industry journals, and both airline and BALPA press releases.

# The exploratory interview

The exploratory interview incorporates the direction of the structured interview, while retaining the freedom to explore issues in greater depth. Its great strength resides in the flexibility it affords as it remains a formal interview where predetermined questions are asked, but researchers are able to use their discretion in pursuing a particular topic. This was extremely useful, especially in the early stages of the project when I required a general understanding of the work and experiences of flight crew.

Interviews were conducted with BALPA officials, flight crew, and members of airline management. The respondents were predominantly middle-aged, professional, highly qualified, and highly educated. The interview is subject to the problem of reflexivity,[6] that is the effect the researcher has upon the phenomenon at issue. In order to compensate for reflexivity, researchers must account for the impression they make on those being investigated. Most interviewees in this study took advantage of the opportunity to inform the researcher, at length, of their opinions. The interviewees in this study reacted to me in the same way as senior management did to Spencer,[7] perceiving a threat from neither the researcher nor the 'project'. Consequently, the majority of respondents seized the opportunity to 'tell it like it is'. I also developed a close relationship with a management respondent at BA. A close relationship was also forged with a senior BALPA representative employed at BA, who was formally interviewed twice during the research (in August 2001 and April 2002). This respondent championed the questionnaire survey when it was proposed at the BALPA Company Council Industrial Forum.

The interviews varied in length but each exceeded 60 minutes, except for the easyJet interviews which lasted on average 30 minutes. Whereas interviews with employees may yield a biased response because interviewees feel uncomfortable about giving away their true feelings about the firm and management, and intimidated by possible adverse consequences, I was justified in my assumption that pilots would demonstrate no such apprehension and I found, as Blain had done in his study of pilots more than 30 years ago, that pilots were unabashed in their response.[8]

The open structure of the interviews removed the possibility of enforcing bias through directed, closed questions. Although occasional interpolations were made to clarify salient or possibly contentious points, questions were asked and interviewees allowed to respond without direction. In all cases, the interviewees were allowed considerable latitude when responding to questions, and only directed if they strayed too far from the focus. All interviews were recorded and later transcribed.

Exploratory interviews were conducted in order to generate ideas to be investigated by other methods.[9] The issues raised in these interviews were explored through focus group discussions and the questionnaire survey. The interviews conducted after the distribution of the survey were performed in order to triangulate the findings from the quantitative data.[10] The schedule, presented in Table 4.1, shows that interviews took place throughout the period of research. This timetable does not include several informal conversations with officials at BALPA, including the Chairperson and several Principal Negotiators, members of the Company Council Industrial Forum following the presentation of the questionnaire in April 2002, and with the new General Secretary, Jim McAuslan, in January 2003.

*Table 4.1* Interview schedule

| Date | Interviewee | Location |
|---|---|---|
| February 2001 | BALPA official 1 | BALPA HQ |
| April 2001 | BALPA official 2 | Liverpool Airport |
| | easyJet pilot 1 – Captain | Liverpool Airport |
| | easyJet pilot 2 – Captain | Liverpool Airport |
| | easyJet pilot 3 – First Officer | Liverpool Airport |
| August 2001 | BALPA official 3 | BALPA HQ |
| | BALPA official 4 | BALPA HQ |
| | BALPA official 5 | Marriot Hotel (Heathrow) |
| | BALPA official 6 | Marriot Hotel (Heathrow) |
| September 2001 | BA flight operations manager 1 | Offices of People in Business (PiB) |
| April 2002 | BALPA official 6 | BALPA HQ |
| | BA flight operations manager 1 | The Pheasant Hotel, Heathrow |
| | BA flight operations manager 2 | Telephone interview |
| | BALPA official 4 | BALPA HQ |
| | BALPA official 1 | BALPA HQ |
| November 2002 | BA flight operations manager 1 | Cardiff Business School |
| July 2003 | easyJet flight operations manager | Telephone interview |
| February 2004 | BALPA official 1 | Telephone interview |
| | BALPA official 3 | Telephone interview |
| October 2005 | BALPA official 3 | BALPA HQ |

## The focus group

The group interview is recognised as a data collection technique to be used in conjunction with, but not to replace, alternative forms of interviews. The academics who coined the phrase 'focus group'[11] used the technique only after collecting a considerable wealth of data, in order to qualify these data already generated by other methods.[12] The method of applying an intensive approach (interviewing) to an extensive context (group) in order to confirm or reject previous analysis proved extremely useful in this study. The findings produced by analysis of the questionnaire survey data were presented at two focus groups for discussion.

In total, five focus groups were conducted during Company Council Industrial Forums at BALPA offices, involving representatives from each of the six sample airlines. Three were conducted in 2002 (February, April, and July) at which data collected from interviews with pilots, BALPA officials, and managers were presented for debate. Initial drafts of the questionnaire content were also presented to the participants during these three focus groups. The suggestions that met with consensus agreement were incorporated into the survey. Two further focus groups, in January and April 2003, involved the presentation of preliminary findings of the questionnaire survey and participants were invited to offer feedback. Focus group participants were all company council representatives, each of whom were keen to participate.

## The questionnaire survey

The questionnaire survey was identified as the optimum method for the collection of attitudinal data from pilots employed at the six airlines. Also, the geographical spread of the bases from which the six sample airlines operated, and the erratic working patterns of pilots, made a comprehensive face-to-face interview schedule extremely difficult to organise. This approach was initially suggested but was rejected by officials at BALPA after extensive discussion. The questionnaire survey collected quantitative data concerning the attitudes of pilots towards airline management and BALPA, together with biographical information. It also allocated space for respondents to comment. Over 30 per cent of respondents elaborated on their responses by including a written comment, which generated a substantial amount of qualitative data. The comments have been used together with data derived from the interviews and focus groups to support the findings of the quantitative data analysis.

Between February and July 2002, three formal presentations were made about the purpose of the study. BALPA's support for the questionnaire survey was given by two separate General Secretaries of BALPA, Chris Darke and Captain John Frohnsdorff. This official support was relayed by the Company Council Chairpersons to members in their airlines. The questionnaire was distributed with a union magazine, *The Log* (October 2002 issue). As a result, only unionised pilots were included in the sample. However, union membership is very high among flight crew. Trade union density surpassed 50 per cent in four of the six sample airlines, and exceeded 40 per cent at the two remaining airlines. Data collected from non-unionised pilots employed at easyJet indicate that their views were comparable to those of their unionised counterparts on issues such as airline management and corporate culture.

Gill and Johnson define the descriptive survey as one which collects data concerning 'the particular characteristics of a specific population of subjects, at a fixed point in time'. They consider it to be most effective when the researcher requires, as I did, information regarding 'job satisfaction; motivation; morale and stress; employee grievances and the satisfactoriness of the means of dealing with them; and the reaction to possible changes in working arrangements'.[13] The questionnaire comprised four distinct sections. The first section, *Airline Management*, collected data concerning the work experience of pilots; their levels of job satisfaction and organisational commitment; changes to work organisation; and their perception of airline management. This first section included ordinal attitudinal indexes and Likert scale questions. It should be noted that questions in each section were designed in such a way that had the respondent ticked all the boxes in a single column then the data would lack consistency and the survey would not have been included in the data set. Whereas a very small percentage of respondents failed to complete certain sections, each survey received demonstrated consistency in response.

In this first section, respondents were asked to identify the presence of HRM content at their airline. The HRM policies and practices included in the survey are indicative of those identified in previous studies.[14] These are presented in Table 4.2.

One of the practices listed in Table 4.2 is specific to the employee group focus of the research and requires further elaboration. Crew resource management (CRM) was introduced with the aim of reducing the frequency of human error accidents and so increasing safety.[15] A principal objective of CRM is to improve communication between crew members. CRM informs pilot selection and influences pilot behaviour onboard the aircraft. It incorporates practices which promote crew interaction and emphasises the importance of communication, problem solving, decision making, interpersonal skills, situation awareness, and leadership.[16] Wright

*Table 4.2* HRM policies and practices included in the survey

| Induction to the firm | Financial participation | Team autonomy |
|---|---|---|
| On-going formal training | Internal promotion | Performance feedback |
| Problem-solving groups | Job enrichment initiatives | Company newsletter |
| Consultation* | Job enlargement initiatives | Suggestion scheme |
| Continuous improvement | Flexible working practices | Employee attitude survey |
| Formal grievance procedures | Service quality training | Total quality management (TQM) |
| Advanced work scheduling | Investors in People (IiP) accreditation | Mentoring arrangements |
| Crew resource management | | |

Note

* Five distinct issues over which consultation took place were distinguished on the advice of employee representatives who claimed the generic term 'consultation' was too vague. The five distinct categories of consultation were identified as: pay and payment systems; work conditions and work safety; training; grievance handling, and personnel planning.

and his colleagues explain the impact of HRM on the performance of the firm in terms of the way in which it motivates employees to use their knowledge, skills, and abilities (KSA) to the optimum level. In these terms, CRM trains pilots to optimise their non-technical KSA.[17] It encompasses a majority of the HRM content stated above in all but name, e.g. formal training, problem solving, consultation, continuous improvement, service quality, team autonomy, performance feedback, suggestion schemes, and TQM.

Legislation introduced by the Civil Aviation Authority (CAA) in January 1995 made CRM training a mandatory requirement for commercial pilots operating in the UK. Pilots flying with European carriers also face regular CRM skill evaluation.[18] Research into pilot response to CRM indicates that the practice has been well received generally.[19] Despite the lack of conclusive evidence demonstrating the positive impact of CRM on accident rates,[20] the significance of CRM within civil aviation and awareness of the need to better evaluate CRM skills is growing.[21]

The first section of the questionnaire begins with an attitudinal index including statements concerning the experience of work. This section required respondents only to tick boxes; no written responses were required. Although starting the questionnaire with a 'personal' section could have created as a natural introduction so that respondents were not put off by more exacting questions, it was believed that beginning the questionnaire by asking for biographical information might have aroused suspicion among the more cynical flight crew and this might have adversely affected the response rate.

The second section of the questionnaire, *The British Airline Pilots Association (BALPA)*, collected data concerning the respondent's attitude towards the Association. This section contained both nominal-level questions (with regard to membership length and representative positions held) and ordinal-level questions (which require an evaluation of BALPA and of trade unions more generally). The trade union representation issues were added to and amended by officials at BALPA. The third section, *The Effect of the Events of September 11th*, required flight crew to evaluate the impact of September 11 on their work experience. Section three included only one ordinal attitudinal index. The fourth section, *Biographical Information*, included 21 questions, nominal, ordinal, and open-ended. Several questions in this section were drawn from Blain's[22] study of flight crew as the issues were still pertinent to the present study.

The content of the questionnaire survey was validated by a lengthy process of critical appraisal and subsequent amendment. Prior to the distribution of the final version, a pilot study was undertaken in which several BALPA flight crew representatives completed the survey. The recommendations made were incorporated into the final questionnaire. The pilot study stage took place in July 2002.

A census of BALPA members at each of the six airlines except BA was undertaken. At the time of distribution, BA employed 3490 pilots who were members of BALPA, almost ten times as many as Britannia, for example. The BA BALPA recipients were selected by stratified random sampling.[23] The BA membership was first organised according to three categories within the BA community: short haul (Heathrow); short haul (Gatwick); and long haul. The membership lists for the three categories were then ordered chronologically by membership date, so that the pilot to join BALPA at the earliest date was first on the list, and the latest to join was last. The sample comprised the first name on the list and every third name thereafter.

In order to maximise the response rate, the explicit support of BALPA was deemed essential as it was hoped that the survey would then be considered legitimate and valuable by the members.[24] As explained above, the questionnaire survey was distributed with *The Log* (Volume 63, No. 5) and a covering letter written by a senior official at BALPA stating the value of the survey to the Association. In the editorial of their specific company newsletters, each of the BALPA Company Council Chairpersons also encouraged recipients to respond.

Frankfort-Nachmias and Nachmias[25] cite the importance of 'inducement to respond' to the response rate of any survey. The inducements to respond to my questionnaire included the endorsement from BALPA officials and representatives, and the appeal of the content to the respondent. As the survey was created over the preceding 18 months, incorporating the concerns of union officials and the pilots who participated in the focus groups, the questionnaire reflected not only the aims of the research but the interests of the parties involved. The questionnaire design is also identified as an important factor affecting the rate of response,[26] and the issue has been treated as of paramount importance. During a focus group in April 2002, several participants opined that the pilots would only make the effort to complete the questionnaire if it was 'professionally designed and presented'. The questionnaire was printed on quality paper with two colours of ink, at considerable extra cost.

Consistent with Fowler's[27] recommendations for enhancing the likelihood of recipient response, each of the questions was prefaced with instructions concerning its completion and its purpose. Also, each of the four sections included a general preamble concerning the purpose of the section and general instructions. Care was taken in the design of the questionnaire to make it 'user friendly'. Finally, the majority of the questions in the questionnaire required respondents to tick one of between five and seven possible responses rather than requiring more time-consuming written responses.

The questionnaire surveys were distributed along with a postage paid return envelope to encourage respondents to reply. On the first page of the questionnaire, the introduction stated that a FREEPOST envelope had been included, and the free postal address was repeated at the end of the introductory text.

Around 20 per cent of the total responses were returned within six weeks of distribution (between October 2002 and November 2002), but

*Table 4.3* Sample and response rate (by airline)

| Airline | *Responses (*n*)* | *Response rate (%)* |
| --- | --- | --- |
| British Airways | 395 | 39.9 |
| Britannia | 124 | 36.8 |
| Air2000 | 60 | 34.3 |
| easyJet | 61 | 29.6 |
| bmi | 95 | 29.3 |
| Go | 27 | 26.5 |
| Total | 762 | 35.6 |

surveys were still arriving in March 2003. Data entry and cleaning of the responses began in October 2002 and was completed in April 2003. It should be noted that although responses from six airlines have been analysed for the purpose of this study, BALPA officials insisted that all affiliates in 24 airlines receive questionnaires in order not to 'exclude' any members. The survey received a total of 1451 responses, with 762 responses from pilots employed at the six sample airlines (see Table 4.3).

## Data analysis

The data collected through the survey were coded and entered into the Statistics Package for Social Scientists (SPSS) (version 11) software package. Analytical techniques used included descriptive analysis, but also ordered least squares (OLS) regression and analysis of variance (ANOVA). These tests are technically inappropriate for use with non-parametric data such as attitudinal responses because such data are not normally distributed. They were only used as an exploratory device in order to discern significant factors and not in a confirmatory manner to 'prove' hypotheses. Thus it is hoped that their use is pardonable, though not vindicated. The data are analysed in the subsequent chapters. The following chapter examines the content and style of HRM at the six airlines and assesses convergence on both dimensions.

# 5    The content and style of HRM in UK airlines

## Introduction

In Chapter 3, HRM was defined as the policies and practices implemented by the firm in the management of its employees (the content of HRM) and the style in which the firm manages its people. The HRM style of the firm is an adaptation of Purcell's[1] management style and is charted along the dimensions of individualism and collectivism: the former is determined by the extent to which management respects 'the feelings and sentiments of each employee and seeks to develop and encourage each employee's capacity and role at work',[2] while the latter refers to the legitimacy afforded the collective by management. This chapter examines convergence on the content and style of HRM in the management of flight crew at six UK airlines.

HRM policies and practices are imitable and as they are commonly held to be the key to unlocking the knowledge, skills and abilities of employees – the elements through which the firm achieves a competitive advantage – there is clearly a motive for firms to converge on the content of HRM in the management of their employees.[3] In the airline industry, not only is there a motive for management to converge on HRM, there is also the pressure from the environment on management to conform to best practice. One might anticipate convergence given the competitive pressures discussed in Chapter 2. Whereas one might expect convergence on HRM content because the associated policies and practices have received a great deal of attention, might we also expect convergence on the less lauded HRM style? Although different terminology is used, studies of management in the US airline industry, for example, have shown marked difference in the HRM style of major carriers.[4]

The purpose of this chapter is, first, to identify the incidence of HRM policies and practices in the management of flight crew at the six airlines and so to assess the convergence on HRM content. The focus will then shift to HRM style at the airlines. The analysis in this and subsequent chapters is performed at three levels. The data are first analysed at the macro (industry) level due to the peculiarities of civil aviation and the implications for its employment practices. Second, as diverse markets within UK civil aviation may explain trends in the data, the data are analysed at the meso (market sub-sector) level. This is crucial so that the attitudes of pilots in airlines with similar operating strategies and facing similar market pressures may be contrasted. The data are then analysed at the micro (firm) level so as to compare airlines both across and within market sub-sectors.

## The sample airlines

The commercial aviation industry in the UK is largely comprised of three market sub-sectors: low cost, full service and charter. Airlines operating in these sub-sectors follow distinctive business strategies which are likely to have implications for employment relations strategies. For example, the low-cost model requires lower standard salaries and a larger performance-related pay component for airline personnel. Therefore, in order to make comparisons between airlines it was imperative to have at least two airlines from each market sub-sector. The low-cost sub-sector is represented by easyJet and Go as these were the two most prominent UK-based low-cost airlines in operation at the time of the research. The full-service airlines are British Airways (BA) and British Midland International (bmi) as these two are the most similar of the full-service airlines. Virgin Atlantic Airways (VAA) was discounted for several reasons. First, it was set up in the late 1980s as a low-cost transatlantic carrier. In this respect it is very different from BA and bmi, both of which emphasise full service and have a heritage that predates the 1960s. VAA opposed recognising BALPA until management were compelled to do so as a result of the Employment Relations Act (1999) and a majority vote in favour of BALPA recognition, whereas both BA and bmi have traditionally recognised BALPA in negotiations. The charter airlines selected were Britannia Airways and Air2000 because they have attracted the greatest amount of media attention, especially with regard to employment relations with flight crew. Also, the HRM style adopted by these airlines is antithetical, and so they present the greatest contrast.

## The content of HRM in UK airlines

Critical accounts of HRM research throughout the 1990s lament reliance on the evidence of a single, potentially biased respondent.[5] Consequently, the study relied on the testimony of flight crew rather than management in determining the content of HRM. In the case of BA and bmi, ancillary data concerning the presence of HRM content were collected from management. The questionnaire survey presented pilots with a list of 26 HRM policies and practices. They were asked to identify which had been implemented in the management of flight crew at their airline.

The results showed that each of the 26 practices was identified by pilots at all of the airlines in the sample. There was, however, considerable disagreement within each of the airlines about the presence of certain practices. This inconsistency, illustrated in Table 5.1, requires further analysis. The majority of pilots at the low-cost airlines recognised 24 of the 26 policies and practices, with mentoring reported by few pilots at either airline, despite the efforts of easyJet management to implement such an initiative to aid socialisation.[6] The majority of pilots at BA recognised 25 of the 26 policies and practices in contrast to 20 acknowledged by bmi pilots. Like flight crew at the low-cost airlines, a large proportion of pilots at both full-service airlines felt that mentoring was absent in the workplace. At bmi and BA, a member of flight operations management also completed a similar questionnaire. There were discrepancies between the responses of the majority of pilots employed at these airlines and the responses of the respective flight operations managers. At bmi, the management respondent claimed that both an employee attitude survey and financial participation had been implemented at the airline for all pilots, whereas over half of the pilot respondents failed to acknowledge financial participation and almost 71 per cent believed that an employee attitude survey had not been implemented. At BA, managers attested to the implementation of mentoring, whereas over 65 per cent of respondents failed to identify this practice. This finding supports the argument that data from management and data from the employee lack congruence,[7] and highlights the need for research to collect comparable data from employees. That is not to say that a managerial perspective is redundant in research of this type, as such data provide an interesting comparison with the reality as perceived by employees.

The greatest difference between airlines in terms of HRM content acknowledgement was found between the charter airlines: 25 policies and practices were recognised by the majority of Britannia pilots whereas the majority of Air2000 pilots identified only 15. The variation between the airlines is perhaps more noticeable if the percentages of pilots who identify each practice are summed, so that an acknowledgement index is generated. It is clear that these practices are more widely perceived at some airlines than at others, as illustrated in the final row of Table 5.1.

*Table 5.1* Recognition of HRM content at the sample airlines

| HRM practice | easyJet | Go | BA | bmi | Britannia | Air2000 |
|---|---|---|---|---|---|---|
| CRM | 100.0 | 100.0 | 100.0 | 100.0 | 100.0 | 100.0 |
| Induction | 95.1 | 96.3 | 90.4 | 88.4 | 84.7 | 88.3 |
| Training | 98.4 | 96.3 | 97.2 | 95.8 | 98.4 | 90.0 |
| Problem-solving groups | 63.9 | 66.7 | 57.5 | 34.7 | 64.5 | 40.0 |
| Consult/pay | 90.2 | 88.9 | 84.1 | 83.2 | 89.5 | 83.3 |
| Consult/work | 80.3 | 81.5 | 79.7 | 71.6 | 83.9 | 75.0 |
| Consult/training | 67.2 | 88.9 | 76.7 | 60.0 | 76.6 | 45.7 |
| Consult/grievance | 63.9 | 81.5 | 77.2 | 57.9 | 77.4 | 43.3 |
| Consult/personnel | 59.0 | 63.0 | 67.1 | 56.8 | 67.7 | 48.3 |
| Continuous improvement | 70.5 | 74.1 | 69.4 | 53.7 | 81.5 | 51.7 |
| Mentoring | 27.9 | 48.1 | 34.7 | 23.2 | 58.1 | 23.3 |
| Formal grievance procedures | 82.0 | 92.6 | 91.6 | 84.2 | 87.1 | 81.7 |
| Advanced work scheduling | 83.6 | 100.0 | 95.4 | 87.4 | 87.6 | 88.3 |
| Financial participation | 86.9 | 96.3 | 81.8 | 49.5 | 31.5 | 90.0 |
| Internal promotion | 93.4 | 100.0 | 91.9 | 82.6 | 90.3 | 93.3 |
| Job enrichment | 70.5 | 77.8 | 69.1 | 55.8 | 66.9 | 61.7 |
| Job enlargement | 67.2 | 70.4 | 64.8 | 56.8 | 62.9 | 53.3 |
| Flexible work practices | 83.6 | 100.0 | 87.8 | 80.0 | 88.7 | 68.3 |
| Service quality training | 67.2 | 70.4 | 56.5 | 51.6 | 66.9 | 38.3 |
| Investors in People | 47.5 | 51.9 | 52.9 | 27.4 | 69.4 | 25.0 |
| Team autonomy | 62.3 | 48.1 | 53.2 | 35.8 | 59.7 | 30.0 |
| Performance briefing | 65.6 | 55.6 | 56.7 | 57.9 | 73.4 | 25.0 |
| Company newsletter | 95.7 | 77.8 | 98.7 | 93.7 | 100.0 | 80.0 |
| Suggestion scheme | 59.0 | 88.9 | 80.0 | 51.6 | 52.4 | 25.7 |
| Employee attitude survey | 55.7 | 85.2 | 91.1 | 29.5 | 67.7 | 18.3 |
| Total quality management | 68.9 | 81.5 | 64.6 | 57.9 | 64.5 | 50.0 |
| Acknowledgement index | 1905.5 | 2081.8 | 1970.1 | 1627.0 | 1951.3 | 1517.8 |

There is clearly a lack of consensus among pilots at the same airlines on the presence of most HRM policies and practices. This finding raises questions about HRM content at the six airlines. For example, does acknowledgement vary according to the age, length of service, rank, or gender of the pilot? Or is variation in recognition a reflection of the ability or commitment of management to implement the policies and practices? If the latter, then why is management at all airlines especially poor at implementing certain practices such as problem-solving groups, mentoring, and team autonomy?

In order to address the first question, ANOVA and Scheffe Multiple Comparison Post Hoc tests were performed on the entire data set. As stated on p. 48, the analysis in this chapter takes the unusual step of applying a parametric test to non-parametric data. The results demonstrate that the practices were no more likely to be identified by pilots of a specific gender or age. There are only a small number of significant differences between the pilots' responses according to their length of service or experience with an airline. These significant differences show no consistent pattern in pilots' likelihood of identifying practices. For example, whereas pilots with over 20 years' experience were significantly *more likely* to acknowledge problem-solving groups than pilots with between six and ten years' experience (at the $p < 0.05$ level), they were also significantly *less likely* to acknowledge induction when compared with pilots with between one and five years' experience (at the $p < 0.05$ level). Therefore, it would be incorrect to assume a consistent positive relationship between the pilot's tenure and acknowledgement of the policies and practices.

There were still fewer significant differences between the responses of pilots of various rank. The differences occurred in response to induction, consultation on pay, financial participation, and employee attitudes survey. Once again, these differences demonstrate no consistent pattern. For example, consultation on pay returned significantly different responses (at the $p < 0.05$ level) from First Officers and Captains, whereas the only significant difference in response to financial participation occurred between Senior First Officers and First Officers (at the $p < 0.001$ level). These results confirm that recognition of HRM content is not a function of any biographical attributes.

A second explanation argues that the variation in recognition of certain policies and practices in a single airline is a function of management inability to implement, or lack of commitment to, the specific practice. The inability of management at all airlines to adequately implement certain practices may be inevitable as a result of the peculiar nature of flight crew work. For example, problem-solving groups are no doubt difficult to organise, given the disparate work of flight crew. If problem-solving groups are arranged, then they are likely to be infrequent. Also, problem-solving groups and team working are likely to mean very little to pilots whose problems are, more often than not, technical in nature and must be addressed as they arise. Moreover, pilots work in pairs (teams) as a matter of course. With regard to IiP, Department of Trade and Industry data reveal that of the six sample airlines, only Britannia is accredited. Despite accreditation at the airline, more than 30 per cent of respondents failed to identify the practice. In analysis of WERS98 data, Hoque illustrates the mediocre impact of IiP accreditation in the workplace, stating that it may have had no effect on the standards of training and development.[8] It is hardly surprising then that so few pilots at the airline acknowledged the practice. Finally, mentoring is extremely difficult to organise as pilots do not work with the same colleagues on a frequent basis. A BA senior manager stated that the only airline in the world that had been able to maintain the necessary level of crew stability to make mentoring possible had been Japan Airlines (*Interview notes*, September 2001).

Whereas all airlines appear to have problems implementing certain policies and practices, it is clear from the analysis that some airlines are better than others in this regard. It is possible that at some airlines, policies and practices have been introduced out of necessity in the management of pilots in order to comply with industry-wide benchmarks, or 'table stakes'.[9] The presence of these practices is no guarantee of management commitment to their success. The data imply a convergence on HRM content among UK airlines, but they also reveal that no such consistency exists between airlines in the ability or commitment of management to these policies and practices.

## The style of HRM at UK airlines

In contrast to HRM content, HRM style is difficult to assess. The approach taken in this study was first to identify facets of work that are important to flight crew, then to assess the way in which these facets have been managed. For example, from interviews with airline management, BALPA officials, and airline pilots it was clear that pilots view themselves as professional workers and wish to be respected as such within the airline.[10] Individualism in HRM style might be expressed by management through genuine recognition of the highly technical, safety-critical and fundamental role of pilots within airline operations. A second way in which management might express individualism, which is essentially a specific subcategory of the first, is through the organisation of work. All pilots fly sectors, whether short-haul sectors of domestic or continental routes or long-haul sectors of more distant international routes. The organisation of flight rosters can have a dramatic impact on the quality of work life for flight crew. In order to assess individualism in HRM style at the six airlines, primary data concerning workload from the questionnaire survey were analysed in conjunction with secondary source information.

Collectivism in HRM style is assessed by examining the industrial relations approach of each airline towards BALPA. In several cases, secondary source data were used in order to assess managerial commitment to collectivism. The assessment by union officials of the relationship between flight crew and management augments these data, and in some cases acts as a proxy for a lack of secondary source information. Like collectivism in management style, collectivism in HRM style is an approach which can be categorised according to Purcell's (1987) continuum. As a result of the Employment Relations Act (1999), each of the airlines in the study has either voluntarily recognised BALPA or has been forced to recognise it via a ballot of flight crew. Thus, collectivism is deemed adversarial or cooperative. The unitary category is included on the HRM schema (see Figure 5.1 on p. 72) in order to illustrate the collectivism of management prior to enforced recognition.

## Low cost 1 – easyJet

easyJet commenced operations on 10 November 1995 with two flights from Luton to Edinburgh and Glasgow. The airline has grown exponentially, carrying just over one million passengers in 1997 compared to almost 33 million in 2006. The airline announced a pre-tax profit of £67.5 million for the financial year ending September 2005 and it has also collected a series of industry awards in recent years including the *Travel Weekly* magazine 'Best No Frills Carrier' award in 2006.

easyJet has been labelled a 'sub-contracting entrepreneurship'[11] and a 'virtual airline' by the management team. It is dependent upon a network of sub-contractors to perform many parts of its operation including delivery of in-flight catering (snacks and drinks sold onboard at the easyKiosk); monitoring of flight schedules and forward planning; baggage handling, check-in and ground staff; provision of fleet maintenance and technical support; and fuel.[12] Although dependence on a network of suppliers is a necessity for a start-up airline, easyJet has shown no indication of bringing these operations in house after more than ten years of operations. Stelios Haji-ioannou, founder of easyJet, has evidently maintained his conviction that 'Market forces eliminate any inefficiencies in the sub-contracting system'.[13]

The company ethos of low cost pervades the entire organisation. The headquarters, easyland, is a bright orange building situated adjacent to the runway at Luton Airport. The head office operates without paper, entirely dependent on information technology. Employee involvement in the airline is ostensibly promoted by the transparency of the communication network, where all company information is available to the entire staff.

Hot-desking and remote working are characteristics of the operation. The easyJet name is associated with the bright orange livery of its aircraft and uniform of its staff. Casual dress is enforced and, except for pilots, the airline has a no tie policy. The company culture is symbolised by the 'orange wheel' mounted above the reception area of easyland. The 'orange wheel', a collage designed by staff, incorporates pictures of all aspects of the airline's operations and represents the inclusive nature of the airline with regard to its employees.

The airline offers passengers 'nothing for free, but everything for sale'.[14] Haji-ioannou likened his airline to a bus company, insisting that passengers on a bus do not expect a free lunch, so neither should his passengers. The comparison of his airline to a bus company, with its regular point-to-point service and inexpensive tariffs, is often cited.

By 2001, the airline was already showing signs of stellar growth and was anticipating the need to employ 140 new pilots every year in order to cope with increasing demand. In his account of the HRM (content) at the airline, Pollock[15] identified the use of sophisticated recruitment and selection policies to select suitable pilots. By running induction and assessment days, the company was able to build a database of pilots who would 'fit in' with the orange culture. Pollock records the views of the then Flight Operations Recruitment Manager who stated that the orange culture was not always popular with pilots who want to 'turn up, fly the plane and not care about anything else'.[16] Thus they were an important target for the 'culturisation' process, part of which involved encouraging existing pilots to take a new recruit out for a drink and introduce them to the easyJet culture. The Business Projects Manager for Flight Operations at the time claimed that 'Pilots, of course, are key staff and their absorption into the culture would always have been an objective'.[17]

HRM content in the management of pilots at easyJet reflects the key components of the high commitment model. First, there has been considerable effort to ensure that pilots conform to the strong company culture. Second, all employees have access to all company information through the airline's intranet. The airline also operates a regular *Pilots Council Newsletter*. Third, a significant component of pilot salaries at the airline is based on sector pay, that is performance-related pay. Finally, the airline operates sophisticated recruitment and selection procedures in order to ensure that the new pilot conforms to the orange culture. Moreover, the majority of respondents to the questionnaire acknowledged 24 of 26 policies and practices.

However, the case of easyJet illustrates the important distinction between HRM content and style. The airline has clearly implemented a raft of HRM policies and practices in the management of flight crew. However, management has also given little 'credence to the feelings and sentiments of employees'[18] by marketing the airline as a 'bus company', thereby implying that pilots are bus drivers and consequently devaluing the safety-critical and highly technical work of flight crew. During an interview with a Flight Operations Manager at easyJet a principal cause of discontent among flight crew at the airline was identified as the 'bus company' image expressed by the airline's founder. The interviewee commented that with this remark the airline had 'shot itself in the foot' in terms of employee relations with flight crew (*Interview notes*, July 2003).

Another way in which management has failed to give credence to the feelings and sentiments of flight crew is by failing to resolve its long-term problem with its scheduling procedures for pilots. This problem has adversely affected the quality of work life for flight crew. During interviews with easyJet pilots in 2001, several interviewees commented on what they perceived to be inadequate work scheduling. A Captain who had formerly flown for a charter airline claimed that his workload had increased substantially since joining easyJet and that he had subsequently sought legal advice about what he perceived to be the 'excessive workload' expected of him by his new employer. He noted of the airline at the time that there were 'desperate staffing issues', and that easyJet did not employ sufficient pilots for its operation. Consequently, he added, pilots were being forced to perform imprudent standby and duty times (*Interview notes*, April 2001). Likewise, another Captain who had previously flown with a different UK charter airline also commented on the 'inadequate roster system' operated by easyJet, which meant that he was 'almost always tired' (*Interview notes*, April 2001). A newly recruited First Officer, flying on a commercial pilots' licence for the first time with easyJet, maintained that although he was 'happy at first', after ten months with the airline he believed that his quality of work life was 'inadequate'. He claimed that pilots at the airline were being 'worked off their feet' and that flight rosters were organised in a reactive manner: 'I object to driving for an hour [to the airport] to fly two sectors. This wastes time and money and saps morale' (*Interview notes*, April 2001).

The gravity of this issue was expressed in August 2002 when the threat of industrial action by easyJet pilots was narrowly averted. A BALPA official responsible for negotiation with easyJet management claimed that similar problems had surfaced in the summer of 2003. At the time of the interview he said he was involved in negotiations with the airline over flight crew working conditions and lifestyle issues. He anticipated 'serious problems' if agreement was not reached (*Interview notes*, February 2004). The interviewee claimed that pilot turnover at easyJet was the highest among the UK airlines that recognised BALPA. In response to a survey conducted by BALPA in 2004, 77 per cent of easyJet respondents indicated that it was unlikely that they would be working at easyJet in the 'foreseeable future' if the remuneration package and conditions remained unchanged. It would seem that management at easyJet have failed to demonstrate commitment to individualism in HRM style, implicitly belittling the professionalism of flight crew and failing to achieve satisfactory work organisation. Indeed, the contrast between the two low-cost airlines in terms of the organisation of pilots' work (see Tables 5.2–5.6) reveals that easyJet pilots were likely to experience a more intense work schedule with fewer days' holiday for comparable pay than their counterparts at Go.

*Table 5.2* Salaries of First Officers (%)

| Airline | <£30,000 | £30,000–49,999 |
|---|---|---|
| easyJet | 0.0 | 100.0 |
| Go | 8.3 | 91.7 |

*Table 5.3* Salaries of Captains (%)

| Airline | £30,000–49,999 | £50,000–69,999 | £70,000–89,999 |
|---|---|---|---|
| easyJet | 10.4 | 44.8 | 44.8 |
| Go | 10.0 | 40.0 | 50.0 |

*Table 5.4* Average number of days off per month (%) (low-cost airlines)

| Airline | None | 1 to 5 | 6 to 10 | 11 to 15 | 16 to 20 |
|---|---|---|---|---|---|
| easyJet | 0.0 | 3.3 | 88.3 | 6.7 | 1.7 |
| Go | 0.0 | 0.0 | 85.2 | 14.8 | 0.0 |

*Table 5.5* Average number of days on standby per month (%) (low-cost airlines)

| Airline | None | 1 to 5 | 6 to 10 | 11 to 15 |
|---|---|---|---|---|
| easyJet | 3.3 | 86.7 | 10.0 | 0.0 |
| Go | 7.4 | 74.1 | 14.8 | 3.7 |

*Table 5.6* Average number of standby days spent flying per month (%) (low-cost airlines)

| Airline | None | 1 to 5 | 6 to 10 |
|---|---|---|---|
| easyJet | 5.3 | 89.4 | 5.3 |
| Go | 29.6 | 66.7 | 3.7 |

Prior to the Employment Relations Act (1999), management at the airline had vehemently opposed BALPA recognition. A BALPA official responsible for members at easyJet commented that an antagonistic relationship between the two sides had persisted since recognition (*Interview notes*, February 2004), and only very recently had the relationship improved (*Interview notes*, October 2005). Until very recently then, collectivism in HRM style conformed to what Purcell labels as 'adversarial'.[19] Whereas the airline scores highly in terms of HRM content, with an acknowledgement index score that exceeds 1900, these data reveal a far weaker emphasis on HRM style (see Figure 5.1, p. 72).

## Low cost 2 – Go

Originally a low-cost subsidiary of British Airways, and commencing operations on May 22 1998, Go became a highly profitable low-cost airline within barely four years. In its final full year as an independent carrier (2001) it reported profits of £14 million, carrying 3.7 million passengers compared with the six million carried by the UK's largest low-cost airline, easyJet. Go was sold soon after Rod Eddington took the helm of the British flag carrier in 2000. As Go represented an image BA wanted to eschew, and that it was competing with BA's own short-haul service, Go was bought out by management, backed by the venture capital group 3i in June 2001, for around £110 million. The airline was later acquired by easyJet in August 2002 for £374 million. In the same year, Chief Executive Barbara Cassani was named UK Entrepreneur of the Year. However, at the time the questionnaire survey was distributed (October 2002) the airline was still operating independently under the Go identity and pilots therefore identified their employer as Go.

Chief Executive Barbara Cassani describes the business strategy of the airline as the '3X+Y formula', whereby '3X means all the basics done cheaply and simply' and 'Y' stands for the quality surprises to which the customer would be treated.[20] For example, cafetiere coffee was served on flights; assigned seating reduced the 'free for all' onboard other low-cost airlines; and free city guide brochures of the destination were offered to customers. The quality of service marked Go's strategy of differentiation. Go was voted the best low-cost airline by *Business Traveller* in October 2001.

The strategy of the airline was essentially low cost but with an added emphasis on service, maximising what Korczynski labels 'customer value' to reflect the service (quality) and tariff (quantity). In an industry where there is intense competition, and where 'customers can increasingly now aim to settle for correct and efficient service outcomes, with a favourable service process as well',[21] customer value is the key to market success.

The rival low-cost airlines in the sample, easyJet and Go, adopted very different competitive strategies. Whereas easyJet adopted a no-frills approach, Go emphasised quality in its low-cost approach. Hence it is *low* frills as opposed to *no* frills. The commitment to a 'no-frills' approach by easyJet has led to its being likened to a bus company, an analogy that has been perpetuated by senior management at the airline to the detriment of employment relations with flight crew. Presciently, Barbara Cassani avoided a similar faux pas when the airline was being named. In consultation with the London design agency HHCL, two names were proposed, Go and The Bus, but Cassani refused to be the 'CEO of a company called The Bus'.[22]

Cassani was also well aware of the problems that a poor relationship with flight crew would pose.[23] An early addition to the senior management team was Ed Winter, a former Chief Pilot with British Airways and veteran of 'tough industrial relations' bargaining with flight crew. He had informed Cassani of the difficulty of managing this group.[24] Consequently, Cassani focused her attentions on generating an industrial relations environment based on mutuality and cooperation rather than adversarialism. From the outset, Go placed great emphasis on recruiting the 'right' people to the organisation. The company's flight crew recruitment policy was focused on evaluating pilots on the merits of their skills *outside* technical competency. In the preliminary development of Go, Cassani generated a 'what-not-to-do' list. Flight crew featured heavily in these guidelines:

> Run the airline in compartments so one part has no idea what's going on anywhere else. Make sure your pilots never meet or talk to commercial people. And vice versa. *My personal bete noire.*[25]

> Hire pilots and not pay attention to their personalities – pilots just fly planes and cabin crew should be hired for good looks, shouldn't they? *Sorry but no; this one really winds me up.*[26]

The airline searched for pilots who would be comfortable with the Go philosophy, a process that was far from easy, as Cassani later reflected:

> In our interviews we wanted to find out what kind of people they were. Many pilots are not accustomed to being interviewed at trendy ad agencies. These interviews were a signal that we wanted flexible people, as much as skilled pilots. Ed and I agreed we wanted pilots to become involved and learn about the whole business, and not to work in cliques. Even during the times when qualified 737 trained pilots were at their most scarce, we turned away people who wouldn't fit in. In some airlines, pilots become too domineering, creating tension with

other colleagues and management ... . I rejected the first Captain we interviewed because she was too concerned about the perks and benefits she was hoping to get. It was a shame because it would have been a nice touch to hire a woman, but she could have poisoned the place with comments about how much better everything was in traditional airlines.[27]

The emphasis Cassani placed on the importance of recruiting the 'right personality' for the Go flight crew community is encapsulated in her assessment of the airline's subsequent success:

Our pilots were a crucial part of our success. We worked through issues, talked and listened openly. It wasn't an age thing. We had some wonderful British Airways retirees who worked hard for us when most of their mates were knocking a ball around the golf course. Similarly, some of our youngest pilots had paid to train for their first commercial pilot's licence from savings and borrowing, and their enthusiasm and energy added to Go's vitality. Others who had worked in a number of airlines knew how bad it could be to work at an airline that endlessly mucked around with your roster, treated you like a number and kept you segregated from the rest of the airline.[28]

The emphasis here is very much on individualism in HRM style. Cassani states that Go was careful to respect the flight and duty times and workload of both flight and cabin crew. In particular, the company sought to respect rosters and never took these for granted:

This may sound like a minor issue, but respecting crew personal time and only infrequently changing their flying schedule goes a long way to achieving good morale. A simple solution, but not that common in airlines. We didn't always get it right. In the early days, when we changed things around because we were making mistakes and late route decisions, we used up a whole heap of favours. I owed them all a lot.[29]

There is congruence between management rhetoric and the reality of flight crew scheduling at Go. The survey data revealed comparable salaries between flight crew at the two low-cost airlines included (see Tables 5.2 and 5.3). However, there were considerable differences in the workload of pilots at each. Tables 5.4–5.6 clearly demonstrate that on average pilots at easyJet were more likely to work on standby days than their counterparts at Go (see Table 5.6). Pilots at easyJet were also likely to have on average fewer days off per month as their colleagues at Go (see Table 5.4).

Clearly then, the organisation of work at Go reflects a greater degree of concern for the feelings and sentiments of flight crew, and therefore a greater commitment to individualism in HRM style, than at easyJet.

Cassani acknowledged the need for a high degree of collectivism and (ultimately) cooperation with trade unions. Another addition to her what-not-to-do list was the following: 'Develop an antagonistic relationship with unions and allow poor employee morale to eat away at your organization. *No thanks, I'd seen enough of that in the US airline industry'.*[30]

Cassani is candid in her reflections on the reasons why unions were recognised at Go from the outset, pointing out that:

> Initially we recognised unions at Bob Ayling's [then CEO of BA] request to avoid industrial strife at British Airways [but] later we embraced the approach because we thought it right to give people the choice of being represented by a union.[31]

An example of the way in which management embraced multiple levels of collective interest representation was the Consultative Group, a discussion forum involving management, employee representatives, and trade union representatives:

> Through the Consultative Group, we included employees in important decisions and we shared how the business was doing – warts and all … . We worked well together on the committee not because we had to but because we wanted Go to be successful and a good place to work. It just seemed like the right way to run a company.[32]

The HRM style at Go is similar to that observed by Von Nordenflycht[33] and Kochan and colleagues[34] in the US airline industry, where high trust and high cooperation between unions and management result in strong mutuality between labour and management. The 'high-quality relationship' they maintain is reflected in the data from Go pilots. In stark contrast to the individualism of HRM style at easyJet, there was a concerted effort to optimise rostering. Clearly the manner in which management dealt with flight crew was very different, emphasising their contribution to the success of the airline. Likewise, in place of the vehement opposition to BALPA witnessed at easyJet, Go sought a cooperative approach to BALPA.

## Full service 1 – British Airways (BA)

The origins of BA can be traced to the birth of civil aviation, following the First World War. On 25 August 1919 its forerunner company, Aircraft

Transport and Travel (ATT), launched the world's first daily international scheduled air service between London and Paris. On 31 March 1924, Britain's four fledgling airlines, Instone, Handley Page, Daimler Airways (a successor to ATT), and British Air Marine Navigation Company, merged to form Imperial Airways, which developed routes to Australia and Africa. Meanwhile, a number of smaller UK air transport companies had begun operating flights. These merged in 1935 to form the privately owned British Airways. Following a government review, Imperial Airways and British Airways were nationalised in 1939 to form British Overseas Airways Corporation (BOAC). Continental European and domestic flights were flown by a new airline called British European Airways (BEA).

In 1972, BOAC and BEA were combined under the newly formed British Airways Board, with the separate airlines coming together as British Airways in 1974. BA, simultaneously with Air France, inaugurated Concorde, the world's first supersonic passenger service, in January 1976. In February 1987 British Airways was privatised and in April 1988 it completed the controversial takeover of British Caledonian, the UK's second largest airline.

British Airways has become one of the world's largest international airlines, flying to 233 destinations in 96 countries. The airline is one of the founding partners of the **one**world alliance (which also includes American Airlines, Aer Lingus, Cathay Pacific, Finnair, Iberia, LanChile, and Qantas). Its franchise partners include British Mediterranean Airways, British Airways CitiExpress, Comair, GB Airways, Loganair, Maersk Air, and Sun-Air (pilots from these airlines have not been incorporated in the questionnaire survey sample). The airline created Go in 1998 in response to the competitive threat of the low-cost airlines, only to sell the operation in 2001.

BA has inspired a wealth of research concerning its employment relations approach,[35] being identified as a benchmark organisation for HRM activity. However, the airline was dogged by industrial action throughout the late 1980s and 1990s.[36] In 1996, the Business Efficiency Programme (BEP) was implemented to save £1 billion. This perpetuated the tradition of unrest at the airline, leading to several costly industrial disputes.[37] The timing of the BEP was far from ideal as it coincided with the airline announcing record annual profits.

This programme of cost savings led to the threat of industrial action by flight crew in 1996. An industrial dispute was avoided. In September of that year, at the behest of Chris Darke, the incumbent General Secretary of BALPA, and Captain Rick Brennan, BA Company Council Chairperson, management consultants People in Business (PiB) were invited to review both the relationship between management and trade union and the attitudes of both parties. A report was made by PiB to BALPA and BA, the primary recommendation being the development of a set of Guiding Principles for the conduct of industrial relations. These principles were generated through a series of workshops involving flight operations management and BALPA officials at which participants 'ripped the skin off one another'.[38] Through a series of often aggressive and acrimonious meetings, BALPA and BA flight operations management developed the Guiding Principles partnership agreement which was signed in January 1997.

Recent studies have shown that the agreement failed to transform adversarial industrial relations between BALPA and flight operations management at BA.[39] The approach of both management and union differs very little from the traditional pattern of adversarial industrial relations.[40] Whereas the airline has not faced a similar threat from pilots to that posed in 1996, a senior BALPA Company Council representative at BA stated,

> We haven't got to the point when we've had the need to ballot members for any sort of action because to date that issue hasn't presented itself. But I think we've come pretty close on a couple of occasions and I think we'll be pretty close in the future.
>
> (*Interview notes*, April 2002)

He commented that whereas the partnership facilitated exchanges between the Company Council representatives and management, it had little meaning for the flight crew community more generally and did not represent a paradigm shift in the attitude of either management or BALPA towards each other:

> I don't perceive any change in the relationship between the management and the wider community ... . Maybe people have changed a little bit, maybe people are a bit more positive about partnership. But I don't think it's changed significantly, there's still a lot of scepticism out there.
>
> (*Interview notes*, April 2002)

The interviewee assessed the partnership on the basis of comparison with other employee groups in the airline, and claimed that pilots' relationship with management was better. However, he inferred an instrumental rationale on the part of management towards their relationship with BALPA and flight crew, whereby management needed to develop a better relationship with pilots because of their industrial strength:

> I guess because of our profile and our role in the airline it's necessary to have a better relationship ... I don't perceive any change directly

from the Guiding Principles in the attempts of management themselves to making a better relationship with the community.

(*Interview notes*, April 2002)

Although the agreement had inspired a moderate change in attitudes, the
new relationship under partnership by no means reflected cooperative collectivism. As the interviewee stated,

> We're [BALPA] getting somewhere, but it's by no means the rela-
> tionship that it could be. And BA are the same. We're both as bad as
> each other. They've got people out there who hate us. You mention
> the word 'BALPA' and they go all cold and shivery.

(*Interview notes*, April 2002)

Whereas the Guiding Principles partnership had slightly improved the
relationship between officials and management, the agreement had meant
very little for the rank-and-file membership. From the secondary data it is
difficult to state conclusively the extent to which management at BA is
committed to individualism in HRM style towards flight crew. Once again,
salary and working conditions were examined as a proxy measure of individualism. It is important when examining the salary and working conditions of pilots at the full-service airlines to allow for the difference
between the respondents at the two airlines in terms of seniority. Seniority
does not affect the low-cost airline pilots. As noted in Chapter 2, seniority
ensures that the salary and working conditions of pilots improve with
tenure. Due to the considerable difference between the full service airlines
in terms of the seniority of flight crew (see Table 5.7), it was necessary to
compare pilots of similar rank and length of service.

The data presented in Tables 5.8–5.11 reflect the responses of pilots *of
the rank of Captain* with *between 11 and 15 years of service* at both BA
and bmi. The data show that pilots at BA were likely to be better paid and
to have a greater number of days off per month than pilots at bmi. Also, BA
pilots were less likely to be required to perform standby duty and, when on
standby, were required to fly less often than their counterparts at bmi.

*Table 5.7* Tenure with present airline (%) (full-service airlines)

| Airline | >1 year | 1 to 5 years | 6 to 10 years | 11 to 15 years | 16 to 20 years | >20 years |
|---------|---------|--------------|---------------|----------------|----------------|-----------|
| BA | 1.3 | 29.6 | 17.3 | 28.4 | 5.6 | 17.8 |
| bmi | 0.0 | 44.7 | 18.1 | 19.1 | 8.5 | 9.6 |

*Table 5.8* Salary (%) (full-service airlines)

| Airline | £30,000–49,999 | £50,000–69,999 | £70,000–89,999 | >£89,999 |
|---------|---------------|---------------|---------------|----------|
| BA | 3.2 | 24.2 | 66.1 | 6.5 |
| bmi | 0.0 | 62.5 | 37.5 | 0.0 |

Note
Percentages based on the response of Captains with between 11 and 15 years' experience.

*Table 5.9* Average number of days off per month (%) (full-service airlines)

| Airline | 6 to 10 | 11 to 15 | 16 to 20 |
|---------|---------|----------|----------|
| BA | 27.4 | 71.0 | 1.6 |
| bmi | 100.0 | 0.0 | 0.0 |

Note
Percentages based on the response of Captains with between 11 and 15 years' experience.

*Table 5.10* Average number of days on standby per month (%) (full-service airlines)

| Airline | None | 1 to 5 | 6 to 10 | 11 to 15 |
|---------|------|--------|---------|----------|
| BA | 39.0 | 54.2 | 6.8 | 0.0 |
| bmi | 0.0 | 56.3 | 37.4 | 6.3 |

Note
Percentages based on the response of Captains with between 11 and 15 years' experience.

*Table 5.11* Average number of standby days spent flying per month (%) (full-service airlines)

| Airline | None | 1 to 5 | 6 to 10 | 11 to 15 | 16 to 20 |
|---------|------|--------|---------|----------|----------|
| BA | 61.1 | 31.5 | 5.6 | 0.0 | 1.8 |
| bmi | 6.7 | 60.0 | 26.6 | 6.7 | 0.0 |

Note
Percentages based on the response of Captains with between 11 and 15 years' experience.

Whereas there is a greater emphasis on individualism in the management of flight crew at BA than at bmi, pilots at the British flag carrier look for comparability internationally rather than nationally, because of the absence of another British airline of the size and global reputation of BA. Doganis[41] illustrates the deficit in pilot salaries at BA compared with many of the US majors and indeed all of the European flag-carrying airlines for which he has data. An alternative indicator of individualism in HRM style at BA is, perhaps, the introduction of a Cabin Service Director onboard aircraft in an explicit challenge to the authority of the Captain. A management respondent at the airline acknowledged the discontent caused by this policy (*Interview notes*, September 2001). Whereas a distinction must be made between the individualism in HRM style at BA and that expressed by management at bmi and easyJet, it is clear that the airline has not emphasised individualism to the same extent as management at Britannia and Go. The position of BA in the HRM style schema (see Figure 5.1, p. 72) reflects the efforts of management to pursue a more positive style in comparison with other UK airlines in the sample, but also the failure on the part of management to successfully demonstrate its commitment to high individualism or inculcate a sense of cooperative collectivism.

## Full service 2 – British Midland International (bmi)

The second full-service airline in the sample is bmi. Despite the differences between the two airlines, it is the most suitable in the UK to compare with BA. Whereas the pilot community was around one-tenth the size of that of BA at the time of the study, the business strategy (as full-service short- and long-haul operators) and longevity of the two airlines were comparable. British Midland Airways became operational in 1964. In 1978, three of the airline's directors purchased a principal shareholding. During the 1980s and 1990s, two European flag carrier airlines, SAS and Lufthansa, purchased a minority shareholding of the airline. In February 2001, the airline was rebranded as British Midland International (bmi) in preparation for its alliance with United Airlines and the commencement of its transatlantic service. Advertised as the UK's second largest full-service airline, it has received 50 industry awards, including 12 consecutive awards for best UK domestic service. In May 2002 the airline received a maximum rating of 5 from *Business Traveller* magazine for its London to Washington service. A member of the Star Alliance, bmi markets itself as an innovator and a quality service provider. The airline is involved in the implementation of industry standards for passenger care, called Airline Passenger Service Commitments (APSC). In 2005, the bmi airline group carried over ten million passengers, with a turnover of £869 million, returning £10 million profit.

The contrast between the salaries and working conditions of pilots at the two full-service airlines indicates a comparative deficit of individualism in HRM style at bmi. The lack of commitment to individualism in HRM style is perhaps best exemplified by the airline's handling of recruitment for its low-cost subsidiary, bmibaby, launched in January 2002. In contrast to the policy adopted by Go to recruit 'new' pilots, bmi transferred mainline pilots to inferior contracts at the new low-cost airline,[42] where they were expected to fly longer hours.[43]

During an interview with a former bmi senior pilot, claims were made that the senior management team shared what was described as a very poor attitude towards pilots (*Interview notes*).[44] A source at BALPA[45] agreed that this negative attitude towards pilots was endemic among senior management and other key members of the management team demonstrated a similar enmity towards flight crew. A senior BALPA official explained that the airline had been subject to continued business pressures that had negatively impacted on the relationship between flight crew and management (*Interview notes*, February 2004). A BALPA survey conducted in early 2004 showed that 65 per cent of respondents at bmi indicated that they did not believe that they would be working for the airline in the foreseeable future.

Collectivism in HRM style was described as typically adversarial by officials at BALPA (*Interview notes*, February 2004). In fact, bmi members of BALPA were balloted for industrial action in 2004. In 2005 members rejected a pay deal offered by the company. Management response was to unilaterally impose the new pay structure for pilots (*Interview notes*, October 2005). The HRM style at bmi is depicted on the HRM style schema (see Figure 5.1, p. 72).

## Charter 1 – Britannia

Britannia is the UK's largest charter airline and was established in December 1961. The airline operates flights from 20 airports to destinations worldwide, including Brazil, Florida, the Maldives, Thailand, and the West Indies. The airline commenced trading as Euravia, operating inclusive tour holidays for Universal Sky Tours. The name Britannia was adopted on 16 August 1964. Britannia became a wholly owned subsidiary of the International Thomson Organization in 1966. In August 1988, Britannia's immediate parent company, the Thomson Travel Group (TTG), purchased Horizon Travel and its airline, Orion Airways, which was integrated into Britannia. In 2000, Thomson Travel Group and Britannia Airways were acquired by the German company TUI Airline Management, formerly Pressuag. TUI Airline Management currently own five European airlines other than Britannia (Britannia (Nordic), Hapag Lloyd, Neos, Corsair and White Eagle Aviation). The company has recently launched a German low-cost airline, Hapag Lloyd Express, as well as selling low-cost scheduled seats on its charter airlines.

The company has received several industry awards, including:

- Travel Weekly Globe Award Best UK Charter Airline (1994–1997 and 2003);
- *Travel Trade Gazette* Top Charter Airline (1991–1999);
- *Travel Bulletin* Top Long Haul Charter Airline (1991, 1997–2002);
- Tommy's Campaign Parent Friendly Best Airline Award (1995);
- *Telegraph* Travel Awards Best Charter Airline (2001 and 2002).

TUI entered the UK low-cost market in March 2004, with its own low-cost subsidiary operated as part of Britannia, which was rebranded as Thomsonfly. The management team of the new low-cost airline followed the lead taken by Barbara Cassani, agreeing recognition with BALPA and the Transport and General Workers' Union (TGWU) prior to commencing operations.[46]

As the first major airline in the UK to receive IiP accreditation (in 1999), Britannia emphasises the importance of its people to the firm. Training and development permeate firm rhetoric. The airline has also led the way among UK airlines in safety developments in the wake of September 11, dispensing with the locked flight deck door policy, which proved deeply unpopular with pilots, in favour of the FlightVu video security for monitoring access to the flight deck.

In January 2003, the airline supplied each of its pilots with IBM ThinkPad X24 laptop computers.[47] This technology offered flight crew easy electronic access to flight manuals required on the flight deck, and was expected to enhance flight safety and efficiency. The new technology offered additional benefits for flight crew who would otherwise have had to manually undertake the complicated calculations for fuel and maintenance efficiency.[48] This initiative, costing the airline an estimated £1 million, highlights the commitment of the airline to flight crew. The on-going commitment to flight crew development was demonstrated in the introduction of Livelink software for existing technology on the flight deck. This enabled flight crew to access the flight briefing system, staff schedules, and security information. Such investment is indicative of a highly technical conception of pilots' work by airline management. It stands in stark contrast to the (non-technical) bus driver image perpetuated by easyJet management.

A claim made by management at the airline is that Britannia has one of the lowest 'leaver rates' in the industry among its pilots, having demonstrated that it is a 'forward thinking organisation committed to investing in quality training for its future pilot workforce' by maintaining its sponsorship programme for pilots with low experience when other airlines abandoned their programmes.[49] As stated above, individualism in HRM style might also be reflected in the salary and working conditions of pilots at these airlines. Due to the effect of seniority on terms and conditions and the considerable difference between the charter airlines in the levels of seniority of flight crew (see Table 5.12), it was necessary to compare pilots of similar rank and length of service so as to eliminate the effect of seniority.

The data presented in Tables 5.13–5.16 concern the salary and working conditions for *Captains* at the charter airlines with *between 11 and 15 years of service* with their employer.

No pilot meeting these criteria at Air2000 reported their salary to be within the highest bracket, in contrast to 10 per cent of their counterparts at Britannia whose gross annual salary was £90,000 or more. Britannia Captains with between 11 and 15 years of service were also more likely to experience a less intense workload (see Tables 5.15 and 5.16) and to have more days off per month (see Table 5.14) than their counterparts at Air2000.

*Table 5.12* Tenure with present airline (%) (charter airlines)

| Airline | 1 to 5 years | 6 to 10 years | 11 to 15 years | 16 to 20 years | >20 years |
| --- | --- | --- | --- | --- | --- |
| Britannia | 22.6 | 1.6 | 30.6 | 12.1 | 33.1 |
| Air2000 | 58.3 | 21.7 | 15.0 | 5.0 | |

Note
Percentages based on the response of Captains with between 11 and 15 years' experience.

*Table 5.13* Salary (%) (charter airlines)

| Airline | £50,000–69,999 | £70,000–89,999 | >£89,999 |
| --- | --- | --- | --- |
| Britannia | 35.0 | 55.0 | 10.0 |
| Air2000 | 0.0 | 100.0 | 0.0 |

Note
Percentages based on the response of Captains with between 11 and 15 years' experience.

*Table 5.14* Average number of days off per month (%) (charter airlines)

| Airline | 6 to 10 | 11 to 15 |
| --- | --- | --- |
| Britannia | 75.0 | 25.0 |
| Air2000 | 100.0 | 0.0 |

Note
Percentages based on the response of Captains with between 11 and 15 years' experience.

*Table 5.15* Average number of days on standby per month (%) (charter airlines)

| Airline | None | 1 to 5 | 6 to 10 |
|---|---|---|---|
| Britannia | 40.0 | 50.0 | 10.0 |
| Air2000 | 0.0 | 71.4 | 28.6 |

Note
Percentages based on the response of Captains with between 11 and 15 years' experience.

*Table 5.16* Average number of standby days spent flying per month (%) (charter airlines)

| Airline | None | 1 to 5 |
|---|---|---|
| Britannia | 47.4 | 52.6 |
| Air2000 | 20.0 | 80.0 |

Note
Percentages based on the response of Captains with between 11 and 15 years' experience.

Thus these data are indicative of a greater commitment to individualism in HRM style at Britannia.

In 2001, Britannia was the only airline other than BA with which BALPA had agreed a formal cooperative relationship. The Association agreed a partnership deal with flight operations management at the airline, despite 'fractious labour relations at the end of 1990s' when Britannia pilots threatened to strike.[50] Pilots from the various European airlines encompassed in TUI formally amalgamated to create the TUI Pilots Group 'to enable them to present a co-ordinated face to the company'.[51] Since then, management and BALPA have liaised over all issues pertaining to a pilot's work at the airline (e.g. rosters, hotel accommodation, transport, and so on). Former General Secretary Chris Darke stated that the agreement with Britannia had surpassed the Guiding Principles partnership between BA and BALPA in terms of the positive relationship that had developed (*Interview notes*, August 2001). An official at BALPA agreed that management at the airline had pursued a cooperative relationship with the Association. He stated that the employment relationship with flight crew had been conducted in the German tradition of industrial relations (*Interview notes*, February 2004).[52] It is clear that management at Britannia has pursued a cooperative approach to collectivism in recent years, having formerly adopted an adversarial approach towards BALPA. Figure 5.1 depicts the position of Britannia on the HRM style schema.

## Charter 2 – Air2000

Established in 1986, Air2000 is the fourth largest leisure airline in the UK and employs over 2300 staff. Its charter and scheduled operations serve 6.6 million passengers per annum, around two-thirds of whom come through its parent company First Choice Holidays. In 2000, Air2000 followed the lead of fellow charter airline Monarch by launching scheduled services from eight UK airports to six of its charter destinations. In 2001, the airline operated from 15 UK and Irish airports to approximately 50 tourist destinations. In October 2003, Air2000 was ranked sixth among European charter airlines on the basis of passenger figures for 2002.[53] Despite weathering the industry crisis after 9/11 better than many of the other UK airlines, the airline dismissed 449 employees (17 per cent) in 2002, and posted a pre-tax profit of £60 million in October that year. In order to save 45 pilot jobs, flight crew at the airline agreed to a 5 per cent pay cut. The airline had threatened to make 77 pilots redundant and demote a further 38 Captains to co-pilot. In June 2003, pilots at the airline threatened industrial action. The 5 per cent pay cut accepted in order to save pilot jobs was agreed, with the provision that it be repaid the following year.[54] Pilots reacted negatively to a pay offer of only 3 per cent whereas they had expected 7.5 per cent in order to bring them back in line with their previous salary.[55]

The employment relationship between pilots and management at the airline has a tradition of animosity. In 1996, it was reported that the turnover of pilots at the airline had reached 28 per cent compared to less than 10 per cent at other charter airlines.[56] Recently, the airline demonstrated low individualism, requesting that its pilots improve their customer service by being more 'flirty and fluffy', entertaining passengers during the flight: 'Pilots have been asked to give better accounts of the flight path and to be a little bit cheeky – for example, instead of "thank you for flying with us" on a night flight, they might suggestively say "thank you for sleeping with us"'.[57]

The airline was vehemently opposed to BALPA recognition until a flight crew ballot in 2000 compelled management to recognise the Association. A BALPA official stated that a former Company Council Chairperson had felt victimised by management, which had created serious difficulties in the relationship between the airline and the Association. The BALPA official identified the airline's approach to collectivism as adversarial (*Interview notes*, February 2004). The position of Air2000 in the HRM style is revealed in Figure 5.1.

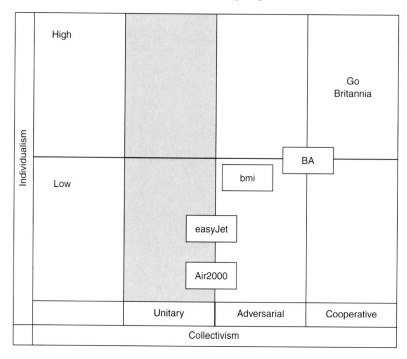

*Figure 5.1* HRM style at the six airlines.

## Summary

The purpose of this chapter has been to examine the HRM content and style at the six sample airlines. Primary data reveal convergence on HRM content in the management of pilots, but significant variation in the ability and/or commitment of the airline to implement the necessary policies and practices. In contrast to the convergence on HRM content, two distinct styles of HRM were apparent. One style involved a high degree of individualism and cooperative collectivism and the other was marked by a dearth of individualism and by adversarial collectivism. These different HRM styles were recorded at airlines operating the same market sector, with the charter airline Britannia and the low-cost airline Go pursuing the former style, while the charter airline Air2000 and low-cost airline easyJet adopted the latter. HRM style is therefore not dictated by the market sub-sector in which the airline competes. The next chapter considers the impact of HRM content and style on job satisfaction among flight crew.

# 6 HRM and job satisfaction

## Introduction

Chapter 5 assessed the content and style of HRM in the management of flight crew at the six sample airlines. The analysis reveals convergence among the airlines on HRM content and two distinct styles of HRM. This chapter and the next assess the impact of HRM on the attitudes of flight crew. A review of the HRM literature, presented in Chapter 3, identifies increased job satisfaction and enhanced organisational commitment as attitudinal outcomes of HRM. Chapter 7 examines organisational commitment among pilots, while this chapter focuses on satisfaction with work. Job satisfaction, defined as the 'positive emotional state resulting from the appraisal of one's job',[1] has attracted considerable attention within the wider field of general social sciences and within employment relations research. It has faced criticism as a 'subjective variable', problematic because it measures 'what people say' rather than 'what people do'.[2]

However, as Freeman points out, 'subjective expressions of job satisfaction are significantly related to future overt behaviour'. For Freeman, job satisfaction is a significant determinant of 'intentions to stay or quit'.[3] Subsequent research by both Akerlof and his colleagues[4] and McEvoy and Cascio[5] among others arrive at similar conclusions. Likewise, on the basis of a study of job satisfaction in Britain, Clark maintains that,

> [w]orkers' decisions about their labour force participation, whether to stay on at a job or quit, and how much effort to devote to a job are all likely to depend in part upon workers' subjective evaluation of their work, in other words on their job satisfaction'.[6]

More recent research, conducted in the UK National Health Service with nurses[7] and general practitioners,[8] supports these findings and demonstrates that lower job satisfaction is associated with an increased incidence of intention to leave. As noted earlier in this book, retention of flight crew is likely to be critical to airlines without a seniority clause due to the anticipated shortage of pilots to meet the present growth in demand for air transportation. As research has linked job satisfaction and propensity to stay with the firm, an analysis of the way in which HRM affects job satisfaction among flight crew is not only of theoretical importance, but is also of significant practical interest to airline management.

## Determinants of job satisfaction

By analysing data from the 1991 British Household Panel Survey, Clark produced a comprehensive list of determinants of job satisfaction. He identifies numerous influential personal and job characteristics, many of which were included in the questionnaire survey of flight crew. Clark finds that the oldest and youngest workers were most likely to be satisfied. The increased likelihood of job satisfaction among older workers is explained in terms of a participation effect, whereby workers in their late fifties and early sixties have a greater opportunity to leave the labour market through early retirement, and thus those in work are more likely to be those satisfied with work. It is probable, therefore, that the 'satisfied older worker' is a 'statistical construct'.[9] The increased likelihood of satisfaction among younger workers, on the other hand, is the result of the novelty of their situation and that they have little or no grounds for comparison. As workers mature, they are able to make this comparison.[10]

Clark also finds that women were more likely to report job satisfaction than men. The 'paradox of the contented female worker', as Bender and Heywood put it, is explained by the lower expectations among women of what the labour market will offer, and who are thus more likely to be pleasantly surprised.[11] Clark elaborates on the reasons for the increased likelihood of satisfaction among women, applying the participation effect once again and arguing that the comparative ease for women to leave the labour market means that there is an increased likelihood of finding satisfied female workers.

In terms of occupation, Clark finds that professionals were more likely to be satisfied with their work (but dissatisfied with their pay) than unskilled workers,[12] and concludes that job satisfaction is not the result of the higher pay that professional work warrants. Clark also finds that higher pay was only weakly correlated with higher job satisfaction because, he explains, pay may compensate workers for the difficulty of their jobs and 'higher paid workers may be doing harder jobs, and therefore will not necessarily be more satisfied'.[13] Similarly, incentive pay was unrelated to job satisfaction.[14] Finally, Clark's results echo those of Idson[15] in finding an inverse relationship between overall job satisfaction and establishment size. Idson previously explained this relationship in terms of the structure and organisation of work: larger establishments were more heavily reliant upon regimentation and standardisation to the detriment of 'worker freedom with regard to how work is done and the scheduling of hours and days'.[16] The determinants of job satisfaction identified by Clark form the analytical framework for the study of flight crew satisfaction.

## Job satisfaction among flight crew

It is common in studies of job satisfaction to measure both overall job sat-isfaction and satisfaction with specific facets of the job,[17] or job satisfac-tion domains.[18] Consequently, this study measured overall satisfaction and the satisfactoriness of with various aspects of work. The questionnaire survey of flight crew required respondents to rate their overall level of job satisfaction using the statement, 'I experience job satisfaction flying with my present employer'. Respondents were asked to rate this statement on a five-point scale of strongly disagree, disagree, neither disagree nor agree, agree, or strongly agree (coded as 1, 2, 3, 4, and 5 respectively). The results by airline are presented in Table 6.1.

On average, pilots were more likely than not to report overall satisfac-tion with their job. Table 6.1 illustrates clear differences between the carri-ers according to the extent of job satisfaction, with a higher than average percentage of pilots satisfied at Go (low cost), Britannia (charter), and BA (full service). It is important to note that these data clearly demonstrate no market sector effect on job satisfaction. Marked differences exist between the responses of pilots employed by airlines in the same market sector. This is best exemplified by the contrast between the responses of easyJet and Go pilots.

*Table 6.1* Percentage of pilots in agreement with the statement 'I experience job satisfaction flying with my present employer' (by airline)

|  | Total disagree | Strongly disagree | Disagree | Neither | Agree | Strongly agree | Total agree |
|---|---|---|---|---|---|---|---|
| Go | 7.8 | 3.9 | 3.9 | 3.9 | 73.0 | 15.3 | 88.3 |
| Britannia | 3.2 | 1.6 | 1.6 | 12.3 | 65.6 | 18.9 | 84.5 |
| British Airways | 13.8 | 3.1 | 10.7 | 16.1 | 56.3 | 13.8 | 70.1 |
| bmi | 24.5 | 7.5 | 17.0 | 20.2 | 45.7 | 9.6 | 55.3 |
| Air2000 | 25.0 | 6.7 | 18.3 | 23.3 | 50.0 | 1.7 | 51.7 |
| easyJet | 35.0 | 11.7 | 23.3 | 18.3 | 40.0 | 6.7 | 46.7 |

Several studies demonstrate that establishment size is inversely related to employee satisfaction. Whereas satisfaction was most widespread among pilots at Go, the smallest airline in the sample on many criteria including the size of the flight crew community, satisfaction was also widespread among pilots at Britannia, the larger charter airline in the sample, and at BA, by far the largest airline in the sample. Thus, in contrast to the findings of Idson,[19] Clark,[20] and Gazioglu and Tansel,[21] establishment size does not appear to have a detrimental effect on the satisfaction of pilots.

The negative association between establishment size and job satisfaction has been explained by the standardisation and regimentation of work in larger organisations, which diminishes worker discretion in their tasks. This does not apply to pilots, whose work is fundamentally autonomous and who work in small groups of two or three people. Therefore, the factors associated with establishment size which are believed to be responsible for decreasing job satisfaction among employees in more usual workplaces are offset by the peculiar nature of flight crew work.

Previous research reveals a U-shaped relationship between satisfaction and age.[22] The data show no such U-shaped relationship between age and satisfaction for pilots (see Table 6.2). Pilots aged 51 years or above were most likely to be satisfied, while pilots of between 46 and 50 years of age were least likely to be satisfied. However, the difference between age categories is not great.

The absence of the U-shaped relationship between satisfaction and the age of the pilot might be a function of inadequate categorisation of the age bands. The category for the youngest pilots is extremely broad and might have included new pilots, whose satisfaction would be inflated because of

*Table 6.2* Percentage of pilots in agreement with the statement 'I experience job satisfaction flying with my present employer' (by age)

|  | Total disagree | Strongly disagree | Disagree | Neither | Agree | Strongly agree | Total agree |
|---|---|---|---|---|---|---|---|
| 21–35 years old | 14.2 | 3.1 | 11.1 | 19.6 | 56.0 | 10.2 | 66.2 |
| 36–40 years old | 19.3 | 5.0 | 14.3 | 13.6 | 56.4 | 10.7 | 67.1 |
| 41–45 years old | 12.7 | 4.8 | 7.9 | 19.8 | 56.4 | 11.1 | 67.5 |
| 46–50 years old | 18.5 | 5.5 | 13.0 | 16.7 | 50.9 | 13.9 | 64.8 |
| >50 years old | 15.8 | 4.6 | 11.2 | 10.5 | 55.3 | 18.4 | 73.7 |

the novelty of the job, along with more experienced pilots, who have developed a more jaundiced view of their work. The influence of rank proved more revealing. The rank of Training Captain is the most senior flight crew position. Training Captains have 'made it', so to speak, and thereby achieved their progression aspiration. Pilots of this rank are also more likely to be older than pilots in the other categories. In contrast, pilots of the rank of First Officer are usually newer to the job and their level of satisfaction liable to be influenced by the novelty of the work.

Consistent with expectations, Training Captains and First Officers were more likely to be satisfied than Senior First Officers and Captains (as Table 6.3 illustrates). Whereas flight crew age and satisfaction do not exhibit the U-shaped model, pilot rank and satisfaction follow this pattern.

Previous studies have shown that gender and satisfaction are linked and that female workers are more likely to be satisfied than their male colleagues. This trend is apparent in the data from flight crew (see Table 6.4). It should be noted at this juncture that in this sample only 5 per cent of respondents were female.

A weak link has been found between salary and job satisfaction in other studies. A similar finding was observed with pilots. High levels of satisfaction were recorded among pilots with the lowest salaries. Pilots

*Table 6.3* Percentage of pilots in agreement with the statement 'I experience job satisfaction flying with my present employer' (by rank)

|  | Total disagree | Strongly disagree | Disagree | Neither | Agree | Strongly agree | Total agree |
|---|---|---|---|---|---|---|---|
| Training Captain | 15.6 | 0.0 | 15.6 | 9.4 | 53.1 | 21.9 | 75.0 |
| Captain | 16.8 | 6.2 | 10.6 | 15.9 | 54.2 | 13.1 | 67.3 |
| Senior First Officer | 16.6 | 3.3 | 13.3 | 22.5 | 52.3 | 8.6 | 60.9 |
| First Officer | 14.1 | 2.9 | 11.2 | 13.6 | 58.7 | 13.6 | 72.3 |

*Table 6.4* Percentage of pilots in agreement with the statement 'I experience job satisfaction flying with my present employer' (by gender)

|  | Total disagree | Strongly disagree | Disagree | Neither | Agree | Strongly agree | Total agree |
|---|---|---|---|---|---|---|---|
| Male | 16.2 | 4.5 | 11.7 | 16.5 | 54.4 | 12.9 | 67.3 |
| Female | 8.6 | 2.9 | 5.7 | 11.4 | 74.3 | 5.7 | 80.0 |

reporting such a salary would have been among the most junior pilots. It is probable that the extent of job satisfaction among flight crew in this category is a result of the novelty of the work rather than a function of salary. Excluding this category, there appears to be a weak positive relationship between salary and satisfaction (see Table 6.5).

As noted in the previous chapter, seniority plays a significant role in the work experience of flight crew at airlines that operate such a system, as it influences workload and salary. Using tenure as a suitable proxy for seniority, the influence of seniority on satisfaction was examined by crosstabulating the data for tenure and overall satisfaction. There appears to be a fairly consistent but unimpressive positive association between seniority and satisfaction (see Table 6.6).

The data reveal weak relationships between personal characteristics and job satisfaction among flight cew. A powerful relationship is apparent between the employing airline and pilot satisfaction. Several of the personal characteristics of pilots that are associated with overall job satisfaction were more prevalent among pilots in airlines where overall satisfaction is most widespread. For example, pilots at BA and Britannia were among the most

*Table 6.5* Percentage of pilots in agreement with the statement 'I experience job satisfaction flying with my present employer' (by salary)

| Gross salary per annum | Total disagree | Strongly disagree | Disagree | Neither | Agree | Strongly agree | Total agree |
|---|---|---|---|---|---|---|---|
| <£30,000 | 0.0 | 0.0 | 0.0 | 7.1 | 78.6 | 14.3 | 92.9 |
| £30–49,999 | 17.5 | 4.5 | 13.0 | 16.7 | 54.5 | 11.3 | 65.8 |
| £50–69,999 | 16.9 | 5.0 | 11.9 | 17.4 | 54.3 | 11.4 | 65.7 |
| £70–89,999 | 14.0 | 4.7 | 9.3 | 16.6 | 59.1 | 10.3 | 69.4 |
| >£89,999 | 14.6 | 2.1 | 12.5 | 12.5 | 51.0 | 21.9 | 72.9 |

*Table 6.6* Percentage of pilots in agreement with the statement 'I experience job satisfaction flying with my present employer' (by seniority)

| Tenure | Total disagree | Strongly disagree | Disagree | Neither | Agree | Strongly agree | Total agree |
|---|---|---|---|---|---|---|---|
| >1 year | 29.4 | 5.9 | 23.5 | 11.8 | 35.3 | 23.5 | 58.8 |
| 1–5 years | 18.2 | 4.9 | 13.3 | 17.4 | 54.8 | 9.6 | 64.4 |
| 6–10 years | 14.0 | 3.4 | 10.6 | 22.3 | 58.1 | 5.6 | 63.7 |
| 11–15 years | 18.1 | 6.7 | 11.4 | 14.5 | 54.4 | 13.0 | 67.4 |
| 16–20 years | 2.1 | 0.0 | 2.1 | 20.8 | 56.3 | 20.8 | 77.1 |
| >20 years | 13.6 | 2.6 | 11.0 | 12.7 | 54.2 | 19.5 | 73.7 |

satisfied pilots in the UK. Also, the respondent composition at BA and Britannia contains a disproportionate percentage of high seniority and high-earning pilots. It is therefore necessary to consider causation. For instance, is it a function of having reached the greatest level of seniority or the highest salary that makes pilots at BA and Britannia more likely to be satisfied? Or is it the case that seniority and salary simply appear to be correlated with overall satisfaction because pilots were more likely to be satisfied at BA and Britannia, and also, incidentally, to be more senior and highly paid? A further crosstabulation of the data for Britannia and BA pilots would seem to refute the former explanation in favour of the latter. There is little consistent difference in the attitudes of pilots of the various seniority categories towards job satisfaction, as Table 6.7 illustrates.

It is clear that the most influential determinant of overall satisfaction is the employing airline. There is considerably less variation in levels of job satisfaction between pilots of a different age, rank, gender, annual salary, and seniority than between pilots at different airlines. It is then interesting to find that airlines where a large percentage of pilots reported overall job satisfaction (Britannia and Go) were the very airlines where there was widespread acknowledgement of HRM content, but crucially also where management was committed to collectivism and individualism in HRM style. In contrast, at the airline where overall job satisfaction was least widespread, easyJet, there was extensive acknowledgement of HRM content, but the HRM style was marked by low individualism and adversarial collectivism. Overall job satisfaction was also limited among pilots at bmi and Air2000, airlines that also adopted adversarial collectivism and a low degree of individualism in HRM style.

*Table 6.7* Percentage of BA and Britannia pilots in agreement with the statement 'I experience job satisfaction flying with my present employer' (by seniority)

|  | Total disagree | Strongly disagree | Disagree | Neither | Agree | Strongly agree | Total agree |
|---|---|---|---|---|---|---|---|
| >1 year | 60.0 | 20.0 | 40.0 | 0.0 | 40.0 | 0.0 | 40.0 |
| 1–5 years | 7.6 | 1.4 | 6.2 | 15.2 | 63.4 | 13.8 | 77.2 |
| 6–10 years | 7.4 | 0.0 | 7.4 | 20.6 | 64.7 | 7.3 | 72.0 |
| 11–15 years | 17.6 | 6.1 | 11.5 | 14.2 | 54.0 | 14.2 | 68.2 |
| 16–20 years | 2.8 | 0.0 | 2.8 | 13.9 | 58.3 | 25.0 | 83.3 |
| >20 years | 10.9 | 1.8 | 9.1 | 13.6 | 55.5 | 20.0 | 75.5 |

## Satisfaction with facets of work

Respondents were also asked to rate the satisfactoriness of constituent elements of their work.[23] For example, the survey of flight crew collected data on: salary, relationship with management, job security, and flight rosters (which is a suitable proxy for 'hours of work' and 'actual work' used by Clark). An additional category of satisfaction with status was added because of its import to flight crew. These items were measured on a four-point scale of highly unsatisfactory, unsatisfactory, satisfactory and highly satisfactory (coded 1, 2, 3 and 4, respectively).

Once again, the data were interrogated for association between the

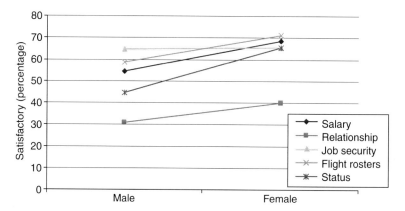

*Figure 6.1* Satisfactoriness of aspects of work (by gender).

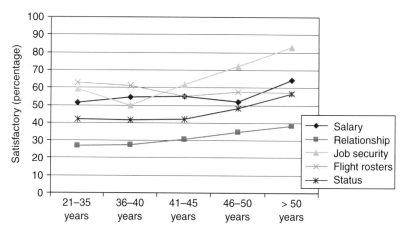

*Figure 6.2* Satisfactoriness of aspects of work (by age).

satisfactoriness of facets of work and the personal characteristics of pilots. Female pilots were more likely to perceive each of the elements of work to be satisfactory than their male counterparts (see Figure 6.1). There is also a positive association between the age of the pilot and the satisfactoriness of each facet except flight rosters (see Figure 6.2). Whereas Training Captains were most likely to feel that each of the aspects of work were satisfactory aside from flight rosters, there appeared to be no consistent pattern according to rank. With the exception of flight rosters, First Officers and Captains were equally likely to view as satisfactory each of the elements of work while Senior First Officers were considerably less likely to find them satisfactory (see Figure 6.3). Finally, there is a fairly consistent

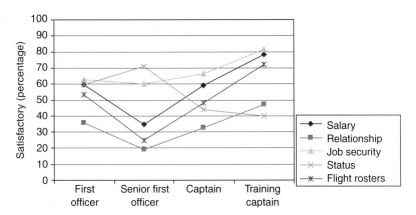

*Figure 6.3* Satisfactoriness of aspects of work (by rank).

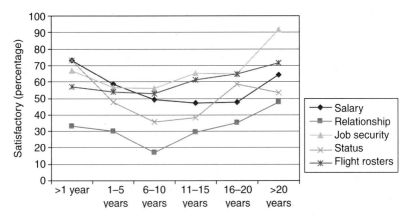

*Figure 6.4* Satisfactoriness of aspects of work (by seniority).

U-shaped relationship between seniority and the satisfactoriness of all aspects of work (see Figure 6.4).

As with overall satisfaction, the influence of the employing airline was sizeable. The majority of pilots at five of the sample airlines reported their salary to be satisfactory. Salary was evaluated to be unsatisfactory by the majority of BA pilots, with over one-fifth of respondents at the airline indicating salary to be highly unsatisfactory (see Table 6.8), despite recording a mean salary higher than that of any airline other than Britannia. In August 2001, there was widespread unrest about salary among the flight crew community at BA. Pilots claimed that their remuneration was out of line with that of pilots at comparable airlines around the world, especially the US 'majors' and the German flag carrier, Lufthansa. Negotiation on pay had been scheduled to take place later in the year, and representatives at the airline were hoping to secure a substantial increase in pay and benefits (*Interview notes*, August 2001). In September 2001, the terrorist attacks in the US paralysed the global civil aviation industry and the effects were most severe for BA among the UK airlines. The airline reported a loss of £200 million as a consequence of the downturn in the industry. Officials at BALPA invoked the Guiding Principles partnership it had agreed with airline management in 1997, postponed negotiations, and espoused support for the airline in the time of crisis. This strategy proved deeply unpopular with flight crew at the airline. The survey was conducted while the resentment about perceived low wages remained prevalent among pilots at BA.

Status was widely felt to be satisfactory among flight crew at Go and Britannia and far less extensively so among flight crew at bmi, easyJet, Air2000, and BA (see Table 6.9).

At these airlines, respondents were inspired to comment on the diminution of flight crew status. For example,

*Table 6.8* Satisfactoriness of salary (by airline)

|  | Unsatisfactory (total) | Highly un-satisfactory | Un-satisfactory | Satisfactory | Highly satisfactory | Satisfactory (total) |
|---|---|---|---|---|---|---|
| Go | 3.7 | 0.0 | 3.7 | 74.1 | 22.2 | 96.3 |
| Britannia | 18.5 | 0.8 | 17.7 | 63.7 | 17.8 | 81.5 |
| bmi | 22.1 | 1.0 | 21.1 | 68.4 | 9.5 | 77.9 |
| Air2000 | 28.3 | 1.6 | 26.7 | 66.7 | 5.0 | 71.7 |
| easyJet | 32.8 | 3.3 | 29.5 | 67.2 | 0.0 | 67.2 |
| British Airways | 65.6 | 22.3 | 43.3 | 31.4 | 3.0 | 34.4 |

*Table 6.9* Satisfactoriness of status (by airline)

| | Unsatisfactory (total) | Highly unsatisfactory | Unsatisfactory | Satisfactory | Highly satisfactory | Satisfactory (total) |
|---|---|---|---|---|---|---|
| Go | 7.4 | – | 7.4 | 66.7 | 25.9 | 92.6 |
| Britannia | 22.6 | 1.6 | 21.0 | 66.1 | 11.3 | 77.4 |
| bmi | 42.1 | 15.8 | 26.3 | 52.6 | 5.3 | 57.9 |
| Air2000 | 46.6 | 8.3 | 38.3 | 51.7 | 1.7 | 53.4 |
| easyJet | 49.1 | 18.6 | 30.5 | 49.2 | 1.7 | 50.9 |
| British Airways | 71.9 | 37.5 | 34.4 | 25.8 | 2.3 | 28.1 |

> Airline management has, in general, become entrenched in its negative attitude to 'bus drivers' in the last 10 years.
>
> (easyJet Captain, QRN[24] 779)

> Part of the problem is the feeling that we are not valued or respected.
>
> (Air2000 Captain, QRN 317)

> Erosion of status must be addressed!! When you have cabin crew earning up to three times more than First Officers, there is a problem!!
>
> (BA Captain, QRN 577)

This response is far from surprising considering the HRM style at these airlines. Both Britannia and Go emphasised the professionalism of flight crew through individualism in HRM style, expressed at the former airline through heavy investment in new technology for pilots and demonstrated at the latter by a commitment to stable rostering and seeking genuine involvement from pilots (see Chapter 5). In contrast, at bmi, Air2000, and easyJet management demonstrated no such commitment to individualism.

The response of BA pilots might be explained in several ways. In researching the impact of perceived external prestige (PEP) on employee attitudes among French managers, Herrbach and Mignonac uncover a positive correlation between PEP and satisfaction: managers were more likely to be satisfied in companies that they perceived to be highly prestigious.[25] At the time of the survey, BA was an airline rocked by the ramifications of 9/11, having already experienced problems prior to the terrorist attacks.[26] It was haemorrhaging passengers to the new-entrant, low-cost airlines. The burgeoning success of the new breed of airline was clearly undermining the dominance and status of the UK flag carrier. Thus, the diminution in pilot perception of external prestige, or of the status of the airline, might have influenced their satisfaction with the status of flight crew in the airline. More likely, perhaps, is that status is intrinsically linked with pay and conditions. Pilots perceive their status to be reflected in their remuneration compared not with that of other employees in their airline, but with that of pilots in what they believe to be comparable airlines. For BA pilots, this would involve a comparison with the remuneration of pilots employed by the continental flag carrier airlines and US 'majors'. As Doganis shows, the average salary of a BA pilot is significantly lower than the average salary of pilots employed at most of the US majors and most European flag-carrying airlines.[27] Also, as noted in Chapter 5, management at the airline had introduced the post of Cabin Service Director onboard its aircraft, a position which many BA pilots felt usurped the authority of the Captain. It is worth noting the widespread perception among flight crew at the airline that erosion of status was a deliberate strategy:

> I am deeply concerned by the willingness of flight crew management to devalue status of flight crew at every opportunity whilst supporting other departments. Also we are treated like kids. Management dictate too many decisions that should lie with the Captain. [Names omitted] strongly give the impression that they despise us. Every decision we hear of serves to reduce our status and empowerment. They project a strong negative view of our position and value. We continuously strive to improve performance. We achieve this but are never recognised or rewarded.
>
> (BA Captain, QRN 91)

> My perception of BA management is that they are purely concerned with tomorrows share price and their own careers without any regard to the long term future of the airline. There is also a constant desire to erode the status and terms and conditions of employment for flight crew.
>
> (BA Senior First Officer, QRN 136)

> The major issue that I have experienced recently is the reduction of status of flight crew within the industry generally. From board to management to cabin crew to cleaner. The work we do is invaluable, but they regard us, to a man, as button pressers. BALPA needs to understand that the one group that can bring down an airline, to its knees, are the pilots. Without them, there is no airline. The length of our training re-enforces this concept! The pilots, not the management, have the power to save my penny share company.
>
> (BA Senior First Officer, QRN 206)

We are fighting an ongoing battle over the status of flight crew. Because we are not 'managers' by title we tend to be regarded as blue-collar train drivers. Addressing this would substantially improve my life for little financial cost to the airline.

(BA Senior First Officer, QRN 323)

The majority of BA pilots also reported the relationship between flight crew and management (henceforth referred to as 'the relationship') to be unsatisfactory (see Table 6.10).

The quantitative data are supported by the qualitative data in terms of the prevalence and content of comments included by BA respondents about management. Indeed, of all the comments made by BA pilots, the largest proportion concerned dissatisfaction with management. For example:

I feel treated like a child, often a condescending attitude put across by managers who seem to put spin on everything! Very few appear to have integrity, the good ones don't seem to last long. I have NO trust in anything Senior Managers have to say – borne out by experience, unfortunately. They have to realise spin doesn't convince anyone for long.

(BA Senior First Officer, QRN 5)

Do flight crew trust their immediate and senior (board level) management to be open and honest, and to act with integrity? Answer for me is no. Also, do flight crew have faith in management in their abilities to efficiently manage the airline for a successful future answer for me is no.

(BA Captain, QRN 233)

*Table 6.10* Satisfactoriness of the relationship between flight crew and management (by airline)

| | Unsatisfactory (total) | Highly un-satisfactory | Un-satisfactory | Satisfactory | Highly satisfactory | Satisfactory (total) |
|---|---|---|---|---|---|---|
| Go | 18.5 | 7.4 | 11.1 | 44.5 | 37.0 | 81.5 |
| Britannia | 26.0 | 5.7 | 20.3 | 69.9 | 4.1 | 74.0 |
| British Airways | 74.4 | 24.4 | 50.0 | 24.9 | 0.7 | 25.6 |
| Air2000 | 86.7 | 30.0 | 56.7 | 13.3 | 0.0 | 13.3 |
| bmi | 88.4 | 51.6 | 36.8 | 10.5 | 1.1 | 11.6 |
| easyJet | 95.1 | 54.1 | 41.0 | 4.9 | 0.0 | 4.9 |

Management is perceived to be untrustworthy, fostering a 'them and us' mentality. I feel that they do not have the best interests of flight crew at heart, and represent other interests, i.e. shareholders, self.

(BA Senior First Officer, QRN 1353)

Once again, there is a gulf between the responses of pilots at those airlines committed to a high degree of individualism and cooperative collectivism and those pursuing a course of adversarial collectivism and a low degree of individualism towards the 'relationship'. The extent of disappointment among Air2000 and bmi pilots approaches 90 per cent, while over 95 per cent of easyJet pilots find the relationship to be unsatisfactory. Comments concerning management at these airlines were by far the most acerbic. The comments made by pilots at Air2000, bmi, and easyJet clearly lament the HRM style at these airlines. At Air2000, comments convey a confrontational relationship between flight crew and management, for example:

Basic morale is poor. Pilots feel they are under attack from management who see cost savings and share price as the only areas of concern.

(Air2000 Captain, QRN 279)

Our management think we should be grateful for a job and should just get on with it. We have a valuable role to play if we are allowed to do it!

(Air2000 Captain, QRN 317)

Likewise at bmi, pilots bemoan their treatment by management which they perceive to be inadequate:

I feel that it did not cover the dichotomy in perceptions between the customer and employer. Namely the customer perceives pilots as highly trained and respected professionals, whereas the management view pilots as a whinging encumbrance, who are overpaid and a drain on the company.

(bmi First Officer, QRN 212)

I work for a very good airline in many ways (safety, training, customer satisfaction). But the way employees are treated is terrible. Industrial relations are at an all time low. There is no trust between pilots and management. We are blamed for much of the airlines inept management.

(bmi First Officer, QRN 145)

The industry is run by accountants, and managers in my company who have no management ability, who are in the positions because they are 'yes-men', and have no integrity.

(bmi Captain, QRN 267)

Management relations at an all time low. Flight safety compromised by poor management. Management practices verge on illegal. Virtually no communication. Very poorly treated by management. Bully tactics endemic. Morale rock bottom.

(bmi Captain, QRN 272)

My opinion of management and my general motivation for this job has only occurred since I joined bmi. I feel how management treat their employees has a significant effect on job satisfaction and morale.

(bmi First Officer, RN 698)

Finally, pilots at easyJet express the most vitriol in their condemnation of the relationship. For example,

Management at easyJet hate pilots.

(easyJet Captain, QRN 690)

In my airline the selection procedure results in a very high standard of professional and motivated crews. Having found these crews it appears the management tries its hardest to ignore the very characteristics they were selected on and treat them with distrust and misinformation. They select highly skilled adults and treat them like children.

(easyJet First Officer, QRN 51)

I have absolutely no faith in the present management of the airline I work for. Their only interest is to satisfy the demands of the shareholders.

(easyJet Captain, QRN 381)

Management are arrogant and avaricious! easyJet is an unhappy place for flight crews and morale is very low.

(easyJet Captain, QRN 152)

I find easyJet management treats everyone with arrogance and contempt!

(easyJet Senior First Officer, QRN 1002)

In stark contrast are the data from pilots employed at Go, the other low-cost airline in the sample. With over 80 per cent of respondents reporting that the relationship was satisfactory, several pilots felt strongly enough about this facet of their work to include a comment. For example,

> I doubt many airlines have been set up, and run like Go, but no other airline had Barbara Cassani as a boss! Ask me the same questions in 12 months time under easyJet management, I do hope I will feel the same.
>
> (Go First Officer, QRN 415)

> It has been the best work decision of my life to join Go. It is a total contrast to the way bmi operate. There is a good flow of information between the management and the air crew – there is a real 'open door' policy and communication is easy with all the senior managers – leading to no 'us and them' atmosphere. Secondly, the rostering is absolutely fantastic – it is stable and the rosterers are human who will help to arrange duties around pilots lifestyles. What a contrast with bmi. I just hope that this will remain when the company is integrated with easyJet.
>
> (Go First Officer, QRN 426)

> Go sadly has now been bought by easyJet. While Cassani was in charge morale, enthusiasm and loyalty were all at a high level. With the advent of the take-over people generally are much less enthusiastic about the future.
>
> (Go Captain, QRN 1142)

At Britannia, the other airline in the sample committed to both individualism and collectivism in HRM style, there was also widespread approval of the relationship, but pilots were not moved to comment on it.

Satisfaction with flight rosters generated similarly extreme responses between airlines. There is consistency between the attitudes of pilots towards their rosters and the actual workloads required of them when the data are compared by market sub-sector. In the low-cost sub-sector, Go pilots were more likely to have on average a higher number of days off per month than their counterparts at easyJet, while they were also less likely to be required to work on their standby days (see Chapter 5). As Table 6.11 clearly depicts, Go pilots were far more likely to report their rosters to be satisfactory than pilots at easyJet. A similar congruence between actual workload and satisfactoriness of the workload exists in the responses of the full-service and charter pilots. BA and Britannia pilots were more likely to report satisfactory rosters, while also reporting a less intense workload, than their counterparts at bmi and Air2000.

*Table 6.11* Percentage of pilots satisfied with flight rosters (by airline)

|  | Unsatisfactory (total) | Highly un-satisfactory | Un-satisfactory | Satisfactory | Highly satisfactory | Satisfactory (total) |
| --- | --- | --- | --- | --- | --- | --- |
| Go | 11.5 | 3.8 | 7.7 | 30.8 | 57.7 | 88.5 |
| Britannia | 23.4 | 4.8 | 18.6 | 59.7 | 16.9 | 76.6 |
| British Airways | 27.4 | 7.1 | 20.3 | 58.9 | 13.7 | 72.6 |
| Air2000 | 68.3 | 33.3 | 35.0 | 30.0 | 1.7 | 31.7 |
| easyJet | 83.6 | 55.7 | 27.9 | 13.1 | 3.3 | 16.4 |
| bmi | 84.2 | 54.7 | 29.5 | 15.8 | 0.0 | 15.8 |

*Table 6.12* Percentage of pilots satisfied with job security (by airline)

|  | Unsatisfactory (total) | Highly un-satisfactory | Un-satisfactory | Satisfactory | Highly satisfactory | Satisfactory (total) |
| --- | --- | --- | --- | --- | --- | --- |
| Britannia | 7.3 | 0.8 | 6.5 | 75.8 | 16.9 | 92.7 |
| easyJet | 19.7 | 8.2 | 11.5 | 67.2 | 13.1 | 80.3 |
| Go | 22.2 | 3.7 | 18.5 | 55.6 | 22.2 | 77.8 |
| British Airways | 33.5 | 5.6 | 27.9 | 59.6 | 6.9 | 66.5 |
| Air2000 | 70.0 | 16.7 | 53.3 | 30.0 | 0.0 | 30.0 |
| bmi | 72.6 | 38.9 | 33.7 | 26.3 | 1.1 | 27.4 |

Finally, job security was widely felt to be satisfactory among pilots at all airlines other than Air2000 and bmi (see Table 6.12). Immediately prior to the survey, pilots at both of these airlines faced job uncertainty. The threat of redundancy loomed at Air2000, while bmi mainline pilots were threatened with transfer to inferior terms and conditions at bmibaby (see Chapter 5).

## The perceived impact of September 11

The questionnaire survey was distributed in October 2002. It was prudent, then, to consider the impact of the events and aftermath of the 9/11 terror-ist attacks on the attitudes of flight crew towards their work. Respondents to the questionnaire survey were asked to assess the impact of 9/11 on various aspects of their work experience. The majority of respondents at four of the six sample airlines felt that 9/11 had detrimentally affected their overall job satisfaction (see Table 6.13).

Pilots also felt that changes implemented to enhance safety were having

*Table 6.13* Pilot perception of the effect of 9/11 on overall job satisfaction (percentage by airline)

| | Total negative | Substantial negative | Negative | No effect | Positive | Substantial positive | Total positive |
|---|---|---|---|---|---|---|---|
| BA | 81.9 | 49.6 | 32.3 | 16.6 | 1.0 | 0.5 | 1.5 |
| Air2000 | 73.3 | 26.7 | 46.6 | 26.7 | 0.0 | 0.0 | 0.0 |
| bmi | 70.5 | 27.4 | 43.1 | 24.2 | 3.2 | 2.1 | 5.3 |
| Go | 66.7 | 18.5 | 48.2 | 22.2 | 7.4 | 3.7 | 11.1 |
| Britannia | 49.2 | 19.4 | 29.8 | 45.2 | 5.6 | 0.0 | 5.6 |
| easyJet | 40.0 | 13.3 | 26.7 | 56.7 | 3.3 | 0.0 | 3.3 |

a negative effect on their experience of work. Concerns about changes to the work environment were expressed by pilots in BA. For example,

> I feel locked in and trapped! … I object personally strongly in not being able to have my wife in the cockpit – surely a more useful/safer resource in the cockpit than being threatened by a hijacker in the cabin.
>
> (BA Senior First Officer, QRN 125)

Interestingly, at easyJet, where flight crew were least likely to report job satisfaction, pilots were also least likely to perceive any detrimental effect of 9/11. One easyJet respondent commented that 9/11 had been used by management to justify cost saving initiatives:

> There is a feeling that many airlines (mine included) have used Sept 11th as an excuse for redundancy and lack of salary increase. Certainly they believe (or it appears) that while there is a pool of available pilots for recruitment why should they bother too much to improve pay and conditions of service. If you don't like it there are plenty more to fill your position.
>
> (easyJet Captain, QRN 228)

A majority of respondents at all airlines felt that 9/11 had detrimentally affected their pay and conditions (see Table 6.14).

To what extent pilots felt that these concessions were actually necessary as a direct result of September 11 is debatable. Comments made by respondents at several airlines indicate a perception that the crisis in the industry was being used by management to justify cost savings: savings that would have been necessary regardless of the crisis following 9/11. For example:

*Table 6.14* Pilot perception of the effect of 9/11 on pay and financial benefits (percentage by airline)

|  | Total negative | Substantial negative | Negative | No effect | Positive | Substantial positive | Total positive |
|---|---|---|---|---|---|---|---|
| Air2000 | 95.0 | 53.3 | 41.7 | 5.0 | 0.0 | 0.0 | 0.0 |
| British Airways | 92.6 | 64.8 | 27.8 | 6.6 | 0.5 | 0.3 | 0.8 |
| Britannia | 82.3 | 32.3 | 50.0 | 17.7 | 0.0 | 0.0 | 0.0 |
| bmi | 78.9 | 34.7 | 44.2 | 20.0 | 0.0 | 1.1 | 1.1 |
| easyJet | 75.4 | 49.2 | 26.2 | 23.0 | 1.6 | 0.0 | 1.6 |
| Go | 55.6 | 14.8 | 40.8 | 44.4 | 0.0 | 0.0 | 0.0 |

> After September 11th management feel they can implement anything because of financial problems within airlines.
>
> (BA Senior First Officer, QRN 1380)

> 9/11 has been used as an excuse, and the way HR issues have been handled during redundancy/restructuring has been without compassion.
>
> (bmi First Officer, QRN 145)

> My opinion of bmi has fallen since 9/11 when demotions and redundancies have taken place without obvious reason.
>
> (bmi Captain, QRN 333)

The industry crisis was widely felt to have negatively impacted on a pilot's relationship with management at all airlines other than those where management had pursued high individualism and cooperative collectivism in HRM style (see Table 6.15). At Britannia and Go, the majority of pilots believed that the crisis had no impact.

The industry crisis has certainly exacerbated pilot dissatisfaction with their relationship with management at several airlines. For example, 80 per cent of bmi respondents who were displeased with their relationship with management felt that September 11 had had a negative impact on the relationship (57 per cent who perceived a substantial negative impact were displeased with the relationship). Similarly, 82 per cent of Air2000 respondents who were unhappy with their relationship with management felt that September 11 had had a negative impact on this relationship (70 per cent who perceived a substantial negative impact were unhappy with the relationship). Interestingly, however, 30 per cent of easyJet respondents who were disgruntled with

*Table 6.15* Pilot perception of the effect of 9/11 on the relationship between flight
crew and management (percentage by airline)

| | Total negative | Substantial negative | Negative | No effect | Positive | Substantial positive | Total positive |
|---|---|---|---|---|---|---|---|
| Air2000 | 93.3 | 80.0 | 13.3 | 6.7 | – | – | 0.0 |
| bmi | 86.3 | 58.9 | 27.4 | 10.5 | 2.1 | 1.1 | 3.2 |
| easyJet | 62.3 | 34.4 | 27.9 | 34.4 | 3.3 | – | 3.3 |
| British Airways | 49.1 | 14.4 | 34.7 | 33.9 | 16.2 | 0.8 | 17.0 |
| Britannia | 31.5 | 4.9 | 26.6 | 53.2 | 15.3 | – | 15.3 |
| Go | 29.6 | 11.1 | 18.5 | 55.6 | 11.1 | 3.7 | 14.8 |

their relationship with management felt that September 11 had had no impact on this relationship.

Unsurprisingly perhaps, 9/11 was perceived to have had a detrimental impact on job security among pilots in the airlines worst affected by 9/11, i.e. the full-service airlines, both of which operated a transatlantic service (see Table 6.16). A large majority of Air2000 pilots also believed that the industry had diminished their job security. As discussed in Chapter 5, pilots at this airline faced redundancy in the aftermath of the crisis and opted for a decrease in pay in order to save pilot jobs. Pilots in the low-cost airlines were significantly less likely to perceive a detrimental impact. Indeed, around 20 per cent of easyJet pilots felt that their jobs had become more secure as a result. This is no doubt a reflection of the unequal effect of the industry crisis. The low-cost airlines weathered the crisis comparatively well, with several European low-cost airlines actually benefiting from their competitors' distress by adopting routes abandoned by the struggling full-service airlines.

*Table 6.16* Pilot perception of the effect of 9/11 on job security (percentage by airline)

| | Total negative | Substantial negative | Negative | No effect | Positive | Substantial positive | Total positive |
|---|---|---|---|---|---|---|---|
| bmi | 95.8 | 77.9 | 17.9 | 2.1 | 1.1 | 1.1 | 2.1 |
| BA | 93.4 | 53.9 | 39.5 | 4.3 | 1.5 | 0.8 | 2.3 |
| Air2000 | 93.3 | 58.3 | 35.0 | 5.0 | 1.7 | 0.0 | 1.7 |
| Britannia | 72.3 | 14.6 | 57.7 | 22.8 | 4.9 | 0.0 | 4.9 |
| Go | 59.2 | 29.6 | 29.6 | 33.4 | 3.7 | 3.7 | 7.4 |
| easyJet | 54.1 | 24.6 | 29.5 | 24.6 | 19.7 | 1.6 | 21.3 |

## Conclusion

This chapter has analysed job satisfaction among pilots in the six sample airlines. Job satisfaction is a commonly cited attitudinal indicator of the impact of HRM, and research has shown a positive link between job satisfaction and employee attitudes such as 'intent to stay'. Pilot retention is, if not already, likely to become a principal preoccupation of airline management due to the anticipated pilot shortage. The job satisfaction of pilots is thus extremely important to successful airline operations.

The attitudes of pilots towards overall job satisfaction and their perception of the satisfactoriness of five aspects of work were marginally influenced by personal and job characteristics such as age, gender, rank, salary, and seniority. However, the extent of job satisfaction among pilots was most powerfully linked with the HRM style of the employing airline. The data analysis sends a clear message that overall job satisfaction and satisfaction with aspects of work was more likely among flight crew employed by airlines where management had pursued high individualism and cooperative collectivism in HRM style. The next chapter considers the other attitudinal indicator of HRM, organisational commitment, and assesses not only the impact of HRM on organisational commitment among flight crew, but also the relationship between organisational commitment and commitment to the trade union.

# 7 HRM, organisational commitment, and commitment to the union

## Introduction

Chapter 6 assessed job satisfaction among flight crew and exposed a powerful nexus between satisfaction and HRM style, whereby more widespread satisfaction among flight crew was found at airlines where management had pursued high individualism and cooperative collectivism. This chapter evaluates a second attitudinal indicator of HRM, organisational commitment. Gaining the commitment of airline pilots is of paramount importance, not only because it makes the airline more likely to retain its pilots but also because pilots who are committed to the organisation are unlikely to be inclined to participate in industrial action, which is liable to be extremely costly.[1]

This chapter also considers the relationship between organisational commitment and commitment to the trade union. It is commonly believed that HRM poses a threat to workplace trade unionism by enhancing the organisational commitment of employees, who are then less inclined to perceive a need for union representation.[2] This chapter examines the impact of HRM on the organisational commitment of flight crew and explores the compatibility of organisational commitment and commitment to the trade union among pilots.

## Organisational commitment

Along with job satisfaction, organisational commitment is an essential component of the way in which HRM 'works'.[3] For example, the most recent model of HRM produced by Purcell and his colleagues avers that HRM policies and practices (the content of HRM), properly implemented, engender greater organisational commitment among employees.[4] More committed to the success of the firm, employees are more likely to demonstrate discretionary effort in their work, or to go the extra mile for the firm, which in turn translates into better firm performance. It is anticipated that, employees committed to the organisation will 'work harder, remain with the organisation and contribute to an organisation being more effective'.[5]

The literature points to four 'bases' of organisational commitment: affective, continuance, normative, and behavioural commitment,[6] although behavioural commitment is often excluded. Meyer and Allen define affective commitment as 'the employee's emotional attachment to, identification with, and involvement in the organisation'.[7] Affective commitment develops as the employee internalises the values and goals of the organisation. Normative commitment also involves an emotional attachment to the organisation, as the employee is inspired by a feeling of obligation to reciprocate in kind the support offered by the firm.[8] These two forms of commitment, based on an emotional or relational bond with the firm, are combined often. Continuance commitment is different in that it involves a rational evaluation of the transactional benefits of remaining with the firm. Continuance or compliance commitment, succinctly defined as 'commitment motivated by necessity',[9] is the result of 'economic or social ties'[10] which bind the employee to the organisation; or, as Meyer and Smith put it, 'continuance commitment is based on the perceived costs associated with discontinuing employment with the organisation'.[11] This form of commitment burgeons as employees amass firm-specific benefits or as the employee develops friendships with colleagues in the firm.

Policies and practices such as Employee Share Ownership Programmes (ESOPs) ought to foster continuance commitment because they offer 'ongoing income that can only be sustained if organizational membership persists'.[12] Whereas we might expect ESOPs to foster continuance commitment, research by Culpepper and his colleagues shows that they can have the opposite effect.[13] Analysing data from US airline pilots, Culpepper and his colleagues find that the presence of high financial value ESOPs were perceived to enable rather than restrict exit from the airline as pilots recognised the benefits of 'cashing in' their shares on departure. Numerous alternative studies show that continuance commitment is not as effective as affective commitment in reducing intention to leave.[14]

## HRM and organisational commitment

The analysis in this chapter focuses on affective commitment because the soft model of HRM, or 'high commitment' model, is believed to enhance this dimension of commitment among employees[15] by offering 'work involvement and a job design that provides scope for responsibility and for self-expression'.[16] Employee involvement has been identified as an important determinant of organisational commitment.[17] In a study of worker attitudes in the UK throughout the 1990s, Gallie and his colleagues arrive at the conclusion that 'if hypothetically nothing else had changed, there would have been an increase in organizational commitment resulting from enhanced participation'.[18]

Employee involvement and participation can be both direct and indirect. Direct involvement is achieved by engaging employees on an individual basis, through 'direct two way communication between workers and management, such as regular meetings between senior management and the workforce, briefing groups, and problem solving groups'.[19] Indirect involvement deals with employees as a collective: involvement is by proxy and achieved by engaging representatives of the workforce. It follows that indirect involvement is more likely to be successful where management in HRM style is committed to cooperative collectivism. There is, then, a theoretical link between cooperative collectivism and organisational commitment. And whereas the methods of direct involvement are closely aligned with HRM content, there is good reason to believe that individualism and collectivism in HRM style moderate the impact of HRM content.

The findings of research reviewed by Meyer and Smith[20] intimate that HRM style remains very important to the successful operation of HRM content. The authors comment that the relationship between HRM and organisational commitment is 'neither direct nor unconditional'.[21] One study they cite finds that the link between HRM policies and practices and organisational commitment was moderated by employee perceptions of managerial intent, specifically by whether it was believed that the implementation of HRM policies and practices was indeed aimed at achieving mutual gains.[22] The authors draw on the findings of research that establishes a link between HRM content and organisational commitment *only* where employees believed that the organisation had implemented HRM in order to attract, retain, and treat fairly the employees in the organisation.[23] Other instances are offered of the failure of HRM content to enhance organisational commitment where employees believed that management had engaged in HRM in order to increase productivity or to comply with employment laws.[24] Through their own analysis, Meyer and Smith find that 'HRM practices might only contribute to employees' affective commitment if they are viewed by employees as evidence of the organization's commitment to them'.[25]

Arguably, the optimum way in which an organisation can demonstrate its commitment to employees is by giving 'credence to the feelings and sentiments of each employee and seek[ing] to develop and encourage each employee's capacity and role at work'.[26] In other words, high individualism in HRM style is a very effective way of conveying the organisation's commitment to employees. The research cited above might plausibly be interpreted as evidence that individualism in HRM style is a powerful moderator of the success of HRM content in enhancing organisational commitment.

Collectivism in HRM style is also likely to contribute to the effectiveness of HRM content in generating organisational commitment. Guest[27] has argued that trade unions provide employees with a 'safeguard or safety net', which goes some way to assuaging the anxiety resulting from changes in the work environment. It is anticipated that employees are more likely to 'buy in' to work initiatives if they are reassured that the union is in a better position to resist managerial prerogative should employees feel that work changes are unfair. In this way, cooperative collectivism reassures employees that they have recourse to an independent organisation, which is able to influence management choice, should they feel aggrieved by developments in the workplace. Moreover, through cooperative collectivism, management confirms its commitment to the employee, encouraging the employee to trust management[28] and buy in to the content of HRM.

Consequently, it is logical to begin with the proposition that collectivism and individualism in HRM style are critical in efforts to enhance organisational commitment among employees. It should be noted that prior research by Guest and Conway has shown that the attitudes of employees towards various aspects of work, including organisational commitment, were most positive in firms where HRM was extensively practised but trade unions were absent.[29] However, airline pilots are unique. In most airlines, BALPA acts as a mediator between management and flight crew because of the disparate nature of flight crew work. In this environment, direct involvement might be less effective and indirect involvement a necessity.

## Airline pilots, HRM, and organisational commitment

Established measures of organisational commitment include pride in organisational membership, a willingness to put oneself out to meet the demands of work, and loyalty to the organisation.[30] Whereas the traditional measure of organisational commitment, the Organisational Commitment Questionnaire, included 15 items, more recent studies have reduced this number considerably. For example, Gallie and his colleagues use a six-item measure of commitment.[31] The questionnaire survey of flight crew adopted this austere approach and included a four-item measure of commitment. The wording of the items in the survey was:

'I am committed to the success of the airline'
'I am willing to put myself out to meet difficult schedules', and
'I am proud to fly for my airline'
'I feel no loyalty towards my present airline' [R]

Respondents were asked to rate the extent to which they agreed with each of these statements using a five-point scale (strongly disagree, disagree, neither disagree nor agree, agree, strongly agree). The responses were coded as 1, 2, 3, 4, and 5, unless they were reverse coded, in which case they were given as 5, 4, 3, 2, and 1, respectively. Reverse-coded questions are identified by [R]. A Cronbach's alpha score ($\alpha = 0.83$) indicated that the commitment statements formed a reliable ensemble, and so factor analysis was used to reduce the four items to a single regression factor (CRF).

In order to evaluate how important HRM style is in determining organisational commitment among flight crew, it was important first to compare the influence of HRM style with the influence of other independent variables that have been identified as significant in predicting commitment. To this end, an OLS regression analysis was performed, wherein the dependent variable was the CRF. It is important to point out that this dependent variable is not strictly appropriate for analysis using the OLS regression because it is not normally distributed. However, this test was only used to delineate significant independent variables, not to measure the exact influence of independent variables. Thus the analysis in this chapter adopts the unconventional approach of using a parametric data test in analysis of non-parametric data.

The independent variables entered in the regression include several personal characteristics that featured in previous studies of organisational commitment such as age and gender, and aspects of work such as gross annual salary and tenure (see Chapter 6 for a description of the bands of age, salary, and tenure). Other independent variables entered into the regression include the rank of the pilot, which was reduced to two categories of command and non-command: Captain and Training Captain were scored '1', while First Officer and Senior First Officer were scored '0'.

In order to assess the differential impact of HRM content and HRM style, the independent variables also included a series of HRM policies and practices designed to enhance involvement, and consequently organisational commitment. The score of '1' was awarded if the pilot acknowledged the presence of the practice at their airline and '0' if the pilot did not. The questionnaire survey required respondents to identify whether they were consulted on five issues: pay, working conditions, training, grievance handling, and personnel planning. Cronbach's alpha indicated that responses to the presence of consultation on these five issues were consistent ($\alpha = 0.87$), and so factor analysis was used to reduce the five issues to a single consultation regression factor.

Finally, HRM style featured as an independent variable in the regression. The analysis in Chapter 5 reveals two distinct styles of HRM. Except for BA, it was very easy to categorise the HRM style at each of the airlines, scoring them either as '0' if they pursued adversarial collectivism and a low degree of individualism, or '1' if the HRM style was marked by cooperative collectivism and a high degree of individualism. The HRM style at BA was scored '0.5', as it occupies a mid point between the highly individualistic and collectivist HRM styles at Britannia and Go (scored 1) and the low individualism and adversarial collectivism of bmi, easyJet, and Air2000 (each of which scored 0).

The regression analysis reveals that four variables are significant in predicting commitment among pilots (see Table 7.1).

In their analysis of organisational commitment in the UK, Gallie and his colleagues find that various initiatives promoting participation, such

*Table 7.1* OLS regression analysis (dependent: CRF)

|  | *Standardised coefficients Beta* |
| --- | --- |
| *HRM content promoting involvement* | |
| Consultation | 0.0277 |
| Continuous improvement | 0.0563 |
| Financial participation | −0.0113 |
| Problem-solving groups | 0.0015 |
| Regular performance briefings | 0.0521 |
| Company newsletter | −0.0020 |
| Suggestion scheme | 0.0810* |
| *Equity of reward* | |
| Satisfactoriness of salary | 0.1113† |
| *Personal characteristics* | |
| Age | −0.0685 |
| Gender | 0.0347 |
| *Aspects of work* | |
| Tenure | 0.1238 |
| Gross annual salary | 0.0685 |
| Command | −0.1486† |
| HRM style | 0.2545‡ |

Notes
Significance levels
* <0.05.
† <0.01.
‡ <0.001.

as quality circles, information meetings, and discussion meetings, are significantly associated with commitment.[32] For flight crew, the suggestion scheme was the only such initiative significantly associated with organisational commitment. A descriptive analysis clearly demonstrates that pilots who were aware of a suggestion scheme at their airline were more likely to agree with each of the positive commitment statements, and disagree with the negative statement, than their counterparts who did not recognise such a scheme (see Table 7.2).

These data are indicative of the widespread desire among flight crew to be more meaningfully involved in the decision-making processes of the airline. The importance of involvement to flight crew was expressed in the comments section of the survey, where many respondents were moved to comment on the perceived lack of pilot involvement at their airline:

> Flight crew have a large level of relevant experience over most operational areas of an airline, yet managers chose to ignore this. Their decisions are made without asking for opinions/advice, and often do not consider what crews would like. Yet when it all goes wrong, the flight crew are expected to sort it out. Hardly a good decision making process.
>
> (Britannia Training Captain, QRN[33] 388)

> There seems to be no consultation, no trust, no consideration for crews (or passengers!), and no grounds for hope for improvement.
>
> (BA Captain, QRN 172)

> Management fail to utilise skills and knowledge of flight crew in solving problems and increasing the efficiency of the airline.
>
> (BA First Officer, QRN 960)

*Table 7.2* Percentage of pilots in agreement with the commitment statements (by awareness of a suggestion scheme)

| | *1 Proud* | | *2 Willing* | | *3 Committed* | | *4 Loyalty* | |
|---|---|---|---|---|---|---|---|---|
| | *Disagree* | *Agree* | *Disagree* | *Agree* | *Disagree* | *Agree* | *Disagree* | *Agree* |
| No awareness | 16.9 | 58.7 | 22.0 | 61.0 | 5.5 | 81.9 | 55.1 | 30.7 |
| Awareness | 9.2 | 78.5 | 14.2 | 76.2 | 3.6 | 88.2 | 66.7 | 20.9 |

Notes
1  I am proud to fly for my airline.
2  I am willing to put myself out to meet difficult schedules.
3  I am committed to the success of the airline.
4  I feel no loyalty towards my present airline.

Tables 7.2–7.6 and 7.8 report only total agreement and total disagreement, omitting the 'neither' response. Therefore percentages might not be 100 per cent.

Management has no interest in what I think/want/do provided I don't break a/c [aircraft] and keep flight deck door shut. I am fed up not being paid world rate for job.

(BA Captain, QRN 1147)

'Feedback managers' seem to exist to pass information down but prevent upward flow of information.

(BA Captain QRN 1266)

Senior management can be perceived as being out of touch or uninterested in workforce issues. ... There is also a feeling that though managers principal task is to implement policy, they actually have little impact up the management chain. Communication ... is poor which naturally affects their vocationally orientated workforce.

(bmi Senior First Officer, QRN 218)

bmi pilot management manage downwards, they do not represent their pilots upwards for fear of their positions. Diodes installed the wrong way round in a circuit.

(bmi First Officer, QRN 320)

My airline is so poor at maintaining dialogue/communications with me, that I found the questionnaire difficult to complete. Not your fault!!

(bmi Senior First Officer, QRN 1148)

Changes to SOP's [standard operating procedures] are often motivated by public perception and fear of litigation, rather than practical flight crew practices. Management make no attempt to seek input from regular line pilots who have the best perception of how changes affect flight safety and crew relations.

(Britannia First Officer, QRN 249)

The only time we see senior management (that above our base Captain) is when there is a campaign on (i.e. the vote on introducing BALPA/pay deals etc.). This is the only time we receive correspondence from them.

(easyJet First Officer, QRN 603)

The satisfactoriness of salary was used as the proxy measure for perceived equity in rewards. The data indicate that perceived equity in rewards has greater explanatory power than any of the HRM policies and practices. This finding is consistent with an equity theory[34] of commitment and congruent with the results of previous organisational commitment research in which the subjects were professional employees. In a study of US lawyers, Wallace found that the perception of the equity of rewards was a significant determinant of organisational commitment.[35] Table 7.3 depicts the difference in attitudes between pilots according to the satisfactoriness of salary. There is a marked difference in attitudes towards commitment between those who consider their salary to be highly unsatisfactory and those who perceive their salary as highly satisfactory. The difference in attitudes between those satisfied and unsatisfied is both less sizeable and less consistent, which suggests that organisational commitment is affected by extreme conceptions of fairness.

It is important to note that whereas the satisfactoriness of salary is significant in predicting commitment among pilots, actual salary is not. The important conclusion drawn from these data is that management is unable to buy the commitment of flight crew.

An unusual finding of the regression analysis is that pilots holding a command position, i.e. of the rank of Captain or Training Captain, were significantly less likely to be committed to their airline than their more junior counterparts, of the rank of First Officer or Senior First Officer (see Table 7.1). Table 7.4 illustrates that the difference between the two groups is not great. However, the finding is odd. It is possible that pilots become cynical about their airline with seniority, whereas more junior pilots have a less jaundiced view of their airline. This point was made of the flight crew community at BA by a manager at the airline. He commented that junior pilots were often more eager and enthusiastic, but as they gained experience they became less enamoured with the airline, or as he put it, 'they joined the dark side' (*Interview notes*, September 2001).

It is clear from the data presented above that HRM content plays some role in determining the attitudes of pilots, through the presence of a

*Table 7.3* Percentage of pilots in agreement with the commitment statements (by satisfaction with salary)

| | 1 Proud | | 2 Willing | | 3 Committed | | 4 Loyalty | |
|---|---|---|---|---|---|---|---|---|
| | *Disagree* | *Agree* | *Disagree* | *Agree* | *Disagree* | *Agree* | *Disagree* | *Agree* |
| Highly un- satisfactory | 22.8 | 55.4 | 33.7 | 58.7 | 6.5 | 83.9 | 58.1 | 30.1 |
| Un- satisfactory | 10.2 | 66.5 | 15.5 | 73.5 | 2.9 | 87.8 | 62.0 | 24.1 |
| Satisfactory | 11.2 | 71.2 | 14.8 | 70.4 | 4.9 | 85.0 | 62.0 | 24.3 |
| Highly satisfactory | 3.9 | 82.4 | 7.8 | 86.3 | 1.9 | 90.4 | 80.8 | 13.4 |

*Table 7.4* Percentage of pilots in agreement with the commitment statements (by command)

| | 1 Proud | | 2 Willing | | 3 Committed | | 4 Loyalty | |
| --- | --- | --- | --- | --- | --- | --- | --- | --- |
| | Disagree | Agree | Disagree | Agree | Disagree | Agree | Disagree | Agree |
| Junior | 8.1 | 72.0 | 15.1 | 70.3 | 2.0 | 88.5 | 66.7 | 20.2 |
| Command | 15.4 | 65.1 | 18.7 | 71.5 | 6.4 | 83.7 | 59.5 | 27.7 |

*Table 7.5* Percentage of pilots in agreement with the commitment statements (by HRM style)

| | 1 Proud | | 2 Willing | | 3 Committed | | 4 Loyalty | |
| --- | --- | --- | --- | --- | --- | --- | --- | --- |
| | Disagree | Agree | Disagree | Agree | Disagree | Agree | Disagree | Agree |
| Adversarial and low | 23.4 | 44.9 | 32.2 | 51.4 | 9.8 | 72.9 | 38.8 | 43.0 |
| Intermediate | 7.9 | 75.4 | 12.0 | 78.3 | 2.0 | 91.9 | 70.5 | 18.1 |
| Cooperative and high | 5.4 | 84.5 | 7.4 | 80.4 | 2.0 | 89.9 | 77.2 | 13.4 |

suggestion scheme in this case. However, it is HRM style that emerges from the regression analysis as the most influential factor predicting organisational commitment (see Table 7.1). Table 7.5 presents a comparison of the attitudes of flight crew according to the HRM style at their airline. A clear and largely consistent difference exists between those carriers committed to collectivism and individualism in HRM style (Go and Britannia) and BA, an airline that has attempted to move away from adversarial collectivism but which has largely failed to demonstrate high individualism in HRM style. However, it is the contrast between these airlines and those in which management has pursued adversarial collectivism and low individualism that is most stark.

These data confirm the impact of HRM style on the extent of organisational commitment among flight crew, and present the resounding message to airline management that organisational commitment was most likely where the trade union was engaged and the pilot was valued as a professional.

## Organisational commitment and union commitment

An important theme in the organisational commitment debate concerns the relationship between commitment to the organisation and commitment to the trade union. It is by enhancing organisational commitment that HRM poses the greatest threat to trade unions,[36] as commitment to the organisation might dissipate the perceived necessity for, or desirability of, the trade union. Guest comments, 'a worker who is committed to the organisation is unlikely to become involved in "industrial relations" or any type of collective activity which might reduce the quality and quantity of their contribution to the organisation'.[37]

Research conducted over 50 years has produced evidence of simultaneous commitment to both the union and the organisation.[38] Theorists have argued that dual commitment stands to benefit the organisation and trade union more than univocal commitment (commitment to one or other) which 'in a unionised workplace may result in an escalation of conflict that backfires, dissuading employees from attaching to either the organisation or to the union and/or motivating dysfunctional workplace behaviours'.[39] For example, in a study of unionised employees at 28 municipal bus companies in the western US, Angle and Perry find that dual commitment was possible, but more likely where the climate between management and union was perceived to be cooperative.[40] Published some 20 years later, the study by Carson and her colleagues supports this view. Whereas they acknowledge the logical reticence by both management and trade union officials to promote commitment to the other (i.e. fear either 'of being taken advantage of' or of 'an erosion of allegiance', or 'suspicion among constituents regarding unexpected cooperativeness'), they argue that failure on the part of either the union or management to promote dual commitment could result in the position of each being undermined.[41] In their study of unionised police personnel at five police departments across the US, Carson and her colleagues find that the attitudes of those who reported dual commitment were more likely to be positive than those of their colleagues who reported commitment to neither union nor organisation or who reported 'univocal' (unilateral[42]) commitment to the union.[43]

The notion that organisational commitment and commitment to the union share a positive correlation[44] has faced criticism. Hoell, for example, argues that several studies of dual commitment throughout the 1990s present little support for the idea.[45] Guest and Dewe[46] and Deery and his colleagues[47] find competing loyalties to the trade union and to management, but no evidence of dual commitment. In contrast to the findings of Angle and Perry and Carson and her colleagues, Deery and his team find that a cooperative industrial relations climate was positively associated with commitment to the organisation, but negatively associated with commitment to the union.[48] Research into the attitudes of unionised employees at electrical power generation facilities in the US leads Hoell to conclude that union commitment and organisational commitment are inversely related.

## Organisational and union commitment among pilots

The questionnaire survey of flight crew did not include all of the measures necessary for a comprehensive evaluation of dual commitment among flight crew. However, the survey did include one of the items Angle and Perry use to measure dual commitment. The survey required respondents to assess the statement, 'You can be a member of a trade union and support management at the same time',[49] using a five-point scale (strongly disagree, disagree, neither disagree nor agree, agree, strongly agree). Responses were coded as 1, 2, 3, 4, and 5 respectively. There was resounding agreement (89 per cent) with this statement among pilots in the sample. It should be noted that this statement only reflects the belief among unionised flight crew that it is possible to be a member of BALPA and support management, not that the two are fundamentally linked.

The survey also included several items that reflect the 'belief in unionism'[50] component of union commitment. These were:

'Flight crew require the assistance of the Association in negotiations with management'
'Without the Association involvement, the airline would be less efficient'
'The involvement of the Association is mutually beneficial for the airline and the individual pilot'

Responses reveal widespread agreement with two of the three items (see Table 7.6). The majority of respondents also agreed with the final statement. Evidently, the preponderance of respondents in the sample valued the involvement of their trade union.

*Table 7.6* Percentage of pilots in agreement with the union commitment statements

|  | *Agree* | *Disagree* |
| --- | --- | --- |
| 'Flight crew require the assistance of the Association in negotiations with management' | 92.4 | 2.0 |
| 'Without the Association the airline would be less efficient' | 54.4 | 19.5 |
| 'The involvement of the Association is mutually beneficial for the airline and the individual pilot' | 75.2 | 10.4 |

Factor analysis was used to reduce the responses to a single union commitment factor. The Cronbach's alpha score for this item confirms that it is a reliable ensemble ($\alpha = 0.71$).

An OLS regression analysis was performed in order to compare the determinants of union commitment with those of organisational commitment. The dependent variable was the union commitment factor. The same independent variables were included as in the organisational commitment regression analysis. Whereas the existence of a suggestion scheme and the perceived equity of rewards (satisfactoriness of salary) are significant predictors of organisational commitment, they are not significant determinants of union commitment (see Table 7.7). However, tenure is positively associated with union commitment. This might be a function of the relationship between tenure and the length of time the union has been established. Pilots with the longest tenure will inevitably be employed by the traditional carriers, i.e. bmi, British Airways, and Britannia, where unions are best established. The table also reveals that HRM style is significantly

*Table 7.7* OLS regression analysis (dependent: union commitment factor)

|  | *Standardised coefficient Beta* |
|---|---|
| *HRM content promoting involvement* | |
| Consultation | 0.0824 |
| Continuous improvement | 0.0491 |
| Financial participation | −0.0059 |
| Problem-solving groups | −0.0345 |
| Regular performance briefings | 0.0443 |
| Company newsletter | 0.0498 |
| Suggestion scheme | −0.0128 |
| *Equity of reward* | |
| Satisfactoriness of salary | −0.0356 |
| *Personal characteristics* | |
| Age | 0.0943 |
| Gender | 0.0279 |
| *Aspects of work* | |
| Tenure | 0.2109† |
| Gross annual salary | −0.0577 |
| Command | −0.0561 |
| HRM style | 0.1653‡ |

Notes
Significance levels
* $p < 0.05$.
† $p < 0.01$.
‡ $p < 0.001$.

*Table 7.8* Percentage of pilots in agreement with the organisational commitment items (by agreement with the union commitment items)

|  | 1 Proud | 2 Willing | 3 Committed | 4 Loyalty |
|---|---|---|---|---|
| 1 Required* | 64.2 | 66.5 | 80.0 | 58.8 |
| 2 Efficient† | 40.0 | 40.6 | 48.2 | 36.5 |
| 3 Mutual‡ | 53.4 | 55.8 | 66.4 | 49.6 |

Notes
* 'Flight crew require the assistance of the Association in negotiations with management'.
† 'Without the Association involvement, the airline would be less efficient'.
‡ 'The involvement of the Association is mutually beneficial for the airline and the individual pilot'.

associated with commitment to the union. The data reveal that pilots at airlines where management has pursued high individualism and high collectivism in HRM style were more likely to agree with the items measuring belief in unionism.

In contrast to the results reported in Table 7.1, it is clear that the variables which significantly predict organisational commitment are largely different to those that predict commitment to unionism. This finding echoes those of Deery and his colleagues.[51] However, in order to assess the relationship between organisational commitment and commitment to the union, responses to the organisational commitment items were crosstabulated with responses to the union commitment items. The data, presented in Table 7.8, reveal the extent of commitment to both the union and the organisation, which far outweighs univocal commitment or commitment to neither.

It is evident that organisational commitment and commitment to the union are not mutually exclusive and indeed pilots were more likely to report commitment to both than to report commitment to one or to neither.

## Conclusion

This chapter has examined commitment among flight crew. The first section examined the determinants of organisational commitment and find that HRM style was significantly and positively associated with the extent of commitment. The data illustrate the benefit of pursuing high individualism and cooperative collectivism in HRM style, as such an approach pays off in enhancing pilots' emotional attachment to their airline. The second section addressed the relationship between organisational commitment and commitment to the trade union. Whereas different factors are significant in determining each form of commitment, commitment to both the union and the organisation is possible. Indeed, crosstabulation of the data demonstrates the greater likelihood of commitment to both organisation and union.

These data reveal a positive and significant association between HRM style and commitment to the union. A priori, this implies that unions stand to benefit in terms of enhanced membership commitment from engaging in cooperation with management. The following chapter examines pilot attitudes towards a cooperative approach on the part of their union and finds that desire for such an approach is not unconditional. It reports a case in which BALPA faced fierce resistance from its membership to its policy of acquiescence with airline management. The next chapter assesses desire for partnership both in principle and in practice.

# 8 Pilots and partnership

## Introduction

The data analysis in Chapter 7 linked HRM style with commitment to both the organisation and the union. On the basis of these data alone we might conclude that the union benefits from HRM style that emphasises individualism and collectivism because pilots who experienced this style of management were more likely to report belief in unionism. Partnership, as an expression of joint commitment by both management and union to work together for the good of all concerned, surely represents the ideal state for BALPA. Ultimately, however, the viability of partnership depends on the attitudes of union members. The attitude of the membership towards partnership is of critical import, especially if members feel that the union is too weak to represent their interests effectively or to make a difference. As a result, rank-and-file members might withdraw their membership, potentially resulting in the demise of trade unionism in the workplace.

Although predating the contemporary partnership debate, Hyman's[1] framework for explaining the effectiveness of the union provides an appropriate analytical tool for understanding the attitudes of rank-and-file members towards partnership. Hyman reasons that union effectiveness is built on legitimacy, autonomy, and efficacy. We might generally anticipate a positive response to partnership by union members if they believe that the gains made in terms of the legitimacy, autonomy, and efficacy of the union as a result of partnership outweigh the losses incurred. Previous studies of union members' attitudes towards partnership have shown a largely sceptical response, as members express the view that partnership meant their union had relinquished these three pillars of effective unionism.

The purpose of this chapter is to evaluate the attitudes of pilots towards partnership. The sample of airlines includes two where BALPA has agreed a formal partnership with management and four where no such arrangement exists. Therefore, it was possible to assess the desire both for partnership in principle (among pilots employed at airlines where no formal partnership exists) and for partnership in practice (among employees employed at airlines with which BALPA had agreed such a relationship). The chapter will begin with an introduction to union–management partnership.

## Partnership

The Involvement and Participation Association distinguishes several components of a genuine partnership, including reciprocal recognition by management and union of each party's legitimate interests; a joint commitment to resolve differences in an atmosphere of trust; transparency and sharing of information; and recognition that unions and employers both gain from delivering concrete improvement to business performance, employee involvement, and terms and conditions. This arrangement between unions and management became increasingly popular in the UK with the election of New Labour in 1997, and has inspired enormous research interest in Britain and in the US.[2] Only recently has research in the UK explicitly evaluated the attitudes of union members towards partnership.

From the generic partnership literature, Roche and Geary[3] propose a binary typology of the advocate and critic perspectives of partnership. Advocates of partnership anticipate a resultant revitalised trade unionism, whereby unions secure a more strategic position within the firm. Ackers and Payne[4] demonstrate no small measure of optimism towards partnership. They predict a 'revamped version of pluralism that sustained union influence',[5] by focusing on the opportunity it offers for trade unions to re-enter the 'mainstream of political and industrial life'.[6] Through compromise and accommodation, the trade union displays itself as a responsible stakeholder. Once it has regained a foothold in political and industrial life, the trade union is able to regulate management decision and strategy making based on the interests of its members.

The potential risk of such an approach on the part of the trade union has been noted by Kochan and Osterman,[7] arguably the most prominent advocates of partnership. The authors emphasise the need for organised labour to '*lead* the coalition', champion the necessary workplace changes, and pursue a more collaborative approach with management. Where unions have traditionally been involved in adversarial relationships with management, partnership represents a significant change in approach and may even 'demobilise' the union. In a US context, for example, Kochan and Osterman[8] caution that this approach may be a 'risky' strategy as the labour movement is then placed at the whim of management. They argue that this risk is outweighed by the dire consequence if organised labour persists with its traditional approach whereby 'management and public policy makers will continue to view labour as a largely negative or, at best, irrelevant force at the workplace and in economic and social affairs'.[9]

The critical perspective of partnership, on the other hand, focuses on the danger of this approach. Kelly[10] has argued that a moderate approach to management is liable to facilitate a demobilisation of union membership, thus diminishing the ability of the trade union to resist management pre-rogative. E.O. Wright[11] restates the position thus:

> because the interests of the workers and capitalists are strictly polar-ized, it is always better for workers to struggle against capitalists – to actively oppose capitalists' interests – than to willingly cooperate. The [cooperative] approach is an illusion … when working-class associations actively cooperate with capitalists, they weaken their capacity for mobilization, and ultimately this invites capitalists to oppose workers' interests.

This critical perspective of partnership is an extension of the incorpora-tion thesis, in which the incorporation of the trade union into the capitalist system is seen as inevitable as a result both of management desire to nullify the threat of trade unionism and of the inherent 'social conditions common to all unions'.[12] Following Michel's 'iron law of oligarchy', incorporation theory holds that trade union officials would inexorably serve their own interests, or at least those of the trade union organisation, rather than those of their members. The interests of the organisation will include the cultivation of 'goodwill or at least the acquiescence of employ-ers and the state'.[13] Thus, the trade union will be incorporated into the bureaucracy of capitalism and become no more than an agent of capital responsible, among other things, for the discipline of its members.[14]

Incorporation of the trade union into management was a central concern for the union officials reported in a study of partnership in the Scottish spirits industry conducted by Marks and her colleagues.[15] The authors describe a partnership agreement where the position of the trade union had become 'precarious' within the firm; where there was evidence of the increased use and enhanced importance of non-union consultative bodies; and where it was clear that 'unless [shop] stewards are able to follow a distinct union agenda, they risk being subsumed within the business-led partnership process'.[16] The authors report the concerns of one union offi-cial who expressed the misgivings of his members about the role of the trade union in the new industrial relationship: 'There are doubts … about our role and being in bed with management'.[17]

Johnstone and his team record similar consternation among employees and found that several participants in focus groups 'were resolutely opposed to the philosophy of management and unions working together'.[18] Respondents felt that as a result of partnership, the union was 'in management's pocket', and they no longer knew where the 'demarcation lines' were between their union and management. This theme emerged in the study carried out by Danford and colleagues[19] into partnership and the high-performance workplace in the aerospace industry. Once again, rank-and-file members relayed their qualms about the new partnership between their union and management and the subsequent disaffection of members from their union: 'I think it should be more "them and us" but it seems to be more "them and them"'.[20]

The response of union members, reported above, largely reflects the concern that their union was being incorporated into management. Applying Hyman's framework of effective unionism, the concerns expressed by members reflect the perception of diminished union legitimacy and autonomy under partnership.

## Pilots and partnership

There is good reason to believe that pilots are more likely to respond positively to partnership. First, pilots are distinct among airline employees as they demonstrate high levels of what E.O. Wright[21] terms structural and associational power. Pilots are highly skilled, possessing extensive generic and specific knowledge that makes their replacement in a strike virtually impossible,[22] and from which they derive significant structural power. In contrast, cabin crew can be trained from novice to operational standard in four weeks, as BA demonstrated during the cabin crew strike of 1997 when replacement staff were drafted in to an army barracks and intensively trained to replace striking employees.[23] As a consequence of their irreplaceability in airline operations, industrial action on the part of pilots has an immediate and substantial impact. The *threat* of industrial action alone by BALPA in 1996 cost BA an estimated £15 million in advance bookings. Also, there is currently an extremely tight labour market for pilots. Indeed, ECA anticipates a dire shortage of pilots in the decade to 2015 as civil aviation continues to grow, and the work of pilots becomes less desirable.[24]

As for associational power, BALPA has high union density in the airlines that recognise it for collective bargaining. At the time of the study, BALPA membership at the two partnership airlines, BA and Britannia, was especially high (exceeding 80 per cent). The Association has also shown that it is not averse to threatening industrial action, as reported in

Chapter 2. As a result of this atypically high level of association among pilots and their structural import there is a more equitable balance of power, or labour parity,[25] between pilots and management. Consequently, pilots 'may be able to mobilize greater power resources and, to some extent, offset the power asymmetry that often impedes effective partnership'; thus this environment provides 'fertile ground' for the development of a successful partnership.[26]

In addition to the power dimension, it has long been established that 'higher grade employees', those more likely to possess higher levels of education 'and thereby [those] able to articulate ideas more easily', will have the greatest desire for the enhanced involvement and participation promised by partnership.[27] Airline pilots are among the most highly qualified, continuously trained and regularly assessed employees in an airline. Thus they possess the faculties to make best use of the advantages offered by partnership and consequently are highly likely to desire such an approach. In addition, pilots have been fiercely defensive of their professional status in the past,[28] and even more so in recent times because of the advances in technology that threaten to proletarianise the work of flight crew. Pilots wish to be seen as professional employees and their union as a professional association. Partnership, as a cooperative relationship between equals, certainly appeals to the image pilots wish to convey.

Finally, it is worth considering the impact union patronage might have on the attitudes of union members employed at airlines with which BALPA has agreed a formal partnership. As partnership at BA and Britannia was driven by the Association it was not the result of proactive strategy on the part of management, and so the union will undoubtedly have made a considerable effort to endorse partnership with the relevant flight crew communities.

## The attitudes of pilots towards partnership

It was possible to assess attitudes towards partnership in principle, among flight crew at easyJet, bmi, Air2000, and Go, where BALPA had not agreed a formal partnership with airline management. Attitudes towards partnership in practice were measured among pilots at the partnership airlines Britannia and BA. In both cases desire for partnership was assessed using the statement, 'The Association should pursue a partnership approach with airline management'. The responses to the statement were recorded on a five-point scale (strongly disagree, disagree, neither disagree nor agree, agree, or strongly agree, coded as 1, 2, 3, 4, and 5 respectively).

Consistent with expectations, the data depict a widely favourable response to partnership in principle among pilots at the four non-partnership

*Table 8.1* Percentage of pilots in agreement with the statement 'The Association should pursue a partnership approach with airline management' (by airline)

|  | Total disagree | Strongly disagree | Disagree | Neither | Agree | Strongly agree | Total agree |
|---|---|---|---|---|---|---|---|
| easyJet | 25.0 | 6.7 | 18.3 | 10.0 | 51.7 | 13.3 | 65.0 |
| bmi | 11.6 | 5.3 | 6.3 | 6.3 | 42.1 | 40.0 | 82.1 |
| Air2000 | 11.9 | 3.4 | 8.5 | 0.0 | 54.2 | 33.9 | 88.1 |
| Go | 15.4 | 7.7 | 7.7 | 3.8 | 53.9 | 26.9 | 80.8 |
| Britannia | 8.8 | 3.2 | 5.6 | 12.9 | 47.6 | 30.7 | 78.3 |
| BA | 31.8 | 15.9 | 15.9 | 13.8 | 39.5 | 14.9 | 54.4 |

airlines (see Table 8.1). Whereas easyJet pilots were less inclined to favour partnership, the response across the four airlines was ultimately positive. In practice, however, partnership derives very different responses from pilots at the two airlines.

The response of Britannia pilots to partnership in practice is congruent with the response of pilots to partnership in principle, with respondents overwhelmingly reporting agreement. Despite a majority of BA pilots favouring partnership, advocacy was around 30 per cent less likely among BA pilots than among their counterparts at Britannia. The analysis in this chapter will now focus on the two partnership airlines, especially BA as the atypical case, in order to explain the response.

Both partnership airlines operate a similar competitive strategy, emphasising service quality that would, prima facie, seem to facilitate partnership. BA has a reputation as a quality service provider, dubbing itself the 'world's favourite airline', while Britannia has secured a series of awards for its service, including recognition as the best UK charter airline between 1991 and 1999 by *Travel Trade Gazette*. Britannia was the only airline in the UK to have achieved Investors in People accreditation (which recognises high-calibre people management and development) at the time of the study. Whereas partnership, as a 'high road' employment relations strategy,[29] corresponds with the competitive strategy at both airlines, neither partnership agreement was introduced as the result of proactive management strategy.

Both partnerships in this study were implemented after many years of hostility between flight crew and flight operations management and each was agreed in immediate response to the threat of industrial action. The Guiding Principles partnership was agreed by flight operations management at BA and officials at BALPA in January 1997 after many years of disharmonious relations between the two. The animosity between BALPA and the airline reached a climax in the summer of 1996 when around 90 per cent of BA members cast an almost unanimous vote in favour of industrial action. The Guiding Principles partnership between flight operations management and BALPA was built on 'ten principles' designed to develop a relationship founded on 'good practice'.[30] Moreover, the partnership was proposed by the consultants People in Business, who had been contracted by BALPA to offer advice on improving the industrial relationship between the union and management.

Similarly, the partnership governing the relationship between BALPA and Britannia was born of industrial conflict and developed largely in response to the 'fractious' relationship between the airline and its pilots at the end of the 1990s.[31] Britannia pilots threatened industrial action in response to the plans made by the parent company, TUI, for the composition of the pilot community of the German-based sister airline. Pilots from the various European airlines encompassed in Britannia's parent organisation formally amalgamated to create the TUI Pilots Group 'to enable them to present a co-ordinated face to the company'.[32] BALPA and management at Britannia agreed to conduct negotiations in the ethos of partnership in 1999. Since then, management and BALPA have liaised over all issues pertaining to the pilots' work at the airline (e.g. rosters, hotel accommodation, transport, and so on).[33] Therefore, management rationale for agreeing a partnership with BALPA at both airlines was in line with a policy of *containment*, intended to constrain future industrial threats, rather than with a choice to *nurture* the relationship with flight crew.[34]

There are, however, several differences between the carriers. First and foremost, there is the substantial difference between the two airlines in terms of the scale of operations and number of pilots employed. The flight crew community at BA was, at the time of the study, around ten times larger than that of Britannia (a similar contrast existed between the airlines in output in available tonne kilometres[35]). The impact of organisational size is well documented. Prior research indicates that organisational size increases bureaucracy[36] and has a detrimental effect on communication within the firm.[37] Consequently, it is possible that the less widespread opinion in favour of partnership in BA was a function of bureaucracy impeding the successful development of a less formal industrial relations structure. It might also be argued that the desire for partnership was reduced because of the difficulty in communicating the ethos of partnership to the large flight crew community in the airline. As it was impossible to test the impact of size any further with the data, the analysis proceeds to consider alternative explanations. One such explanation was shared by a manager at the airline and a senior union representative.

During separate interviews both union and management respondents attributed differences of opinion between pilots about partnership to the tenure of the pilot. A BALPA representative claimed that the partnership operated effectively at the highest level between the Company Council and flight operations management at BA:

> I don't think it actually helps our own community's perspective of what's going on, what the activity is. You get all sorts of views out in the community, but it's important for the relationship where things are happening and where exchanges are taking place, I don't think it's relevant on the street. ... The importance of partnership is in the relationship itself with management.
>
> (*Interview notes*, April 2002)

He added that at the time of the interview there were insurmountable barriers preventing belief in the ethos of partnership among the wider BA flight crew community, namely the dire labour relations climate prior to the agreement. He stated that his colleagues in the BA flight crew community misconstrued social partnership, and believed it meant pilots and management becoming 'mates and going for a pint together on a Friday night' (*Interview* notes, April 2002). As the majority of management and flight crew felt genuine animosity towards one another, partnership thus defined would not take root. Both union representatives and management (mistakenly) attributed negative attitudes to more experienced pilots. For example, a BALPA representative argued that as older BA pilots with experience of the 'bad old days' before partnership were retiring, there would be a chance to cultivate partnership with younger pilots:

> Because of the turnover we've got, we've now got a lot more old fashioned thinkers retiring. There is an opportunity with a lot of younger minds around to build from a point where they're not already set in stone. Their thoughts on the relationship aren't well founded or they don't go back 25 years of bad history or bad blood that they can't see the light at the end of the tunnel perhaps and buy in more to the partnership.
>
> (*Interview notes*, April 2002)

A BA manager, interviewed in September 2001, shared this view. He stated that when junior pilots joined they were proud to fly for the airline, enthusiastic about their work, and receptive to management input. He suggested that the history of animosity between flight crew and management tainted the views of more senior pilots. He added that the partnership would be better received by junior and younger pilots than by pilots with experience of the 'bad old days' before the Guiding Principles agreement signed in 1997 (*Interview notes*, September 2001). Both participants held the view that objection to partnership was largely the preserve of longer-serving or more senior pilots, those having experienced the traditional antagonism of the industrial relationship between flight crew and management before the partnership. They suggested that these pilots were inevitably less likely to advocate a collaborative approach based on experience. More junior pilots without this experience would be more likely to buy into the ethos of partnership. In order to further explore the proposition that tenure and desire for partnership among BA pilots were negatively associated, the data from pilots at the airline were isolated and analysed separately.

Attitudes towards partnership among pilots who joined the airline after the introduction of the Guiding Principles (those with less than six years' experience at the time of the survey) and those in post prior to the partnership agreement (with six or more years' experience) were compared. The results show a small difference between the two groups consistent with the speculation by management and union representatives. This variation is, however, insufficient to explain the lack of overall desire for partnership at the airline (see Table 8.2).

Moving from speculation to theory, previous research into the attitudes of union members towards partnership has reported a largely negative response, with concerns expressed about the autonomy and legitimacy, and ultimately the effectiveness, of the union under partnership. Pilots enjoy a high level of industrial power. Consequently, the effectiveness of the union under partnership is likely to come in for particular scrutiny by pilots who will be aware that their interests might be better served by an adversarial strategy.[38] Whereas the principle of partnership is congruent with the image pilots wish to convey, it is unlikely to be popular in practice if it leads to a

*Table 8.2* Percentage of pilots in agreement with the statement 'The Association should pursue a partnership approach with airline management' (by tenure)

|  | Total disagree | Strongly disagree | Disagree | Neither | Agree | Strongly agree | Total agree |
|---|---|---|---|---|---|---|---|
| Less than 6 years | 27.3 | 11.6 | 15.7 | 15.7 | 43.8 | 13.2 | 57.0 |
| 6 or more years | 33.9 | 17.9 | 16.0 | 13.1 | 37.3 | 15.7 | 53.0 |

diminution of union effectiveness. In practice, advocacy of partnership is likely to be contingent upon the cost benefit analysis identified above, where a positive response is more likely when, on balance, the pilot feels that the union has benefited more in terms of legitimacy, autonomy, and efficacy than it has lost as a result of partnership. Therefore, an alternative explanation of the limited desire for partnership among BA flight crew focuses on the perceived effectiveness of the Association under partnership.

Several measures of the perception of BALPA efficacy were included in the questionnaire survey. At a general level respondents were asked to evaluate the statement, 'The Association effectively represents my interests within the airline' along the same scale as the partnership statement (see p. 114). This is referred to as the efficacy statement. Respondents were also required to rate the satisfactoriness of BALPA efficacy in representation on 11 issues determined by the researcher and officials at BALPA: improving pay, legal protection, scheduling agreements, support when problems arise, improving industrial benefits, involvement in European/international matters, professional services, financial services, employment services, technical support, and improving health and safety. These issues were assessed on a four-point scale (highly unsatisfactory, unsatisfactory, satisfactory, and highly satisfactory, coded 1, 2, 3 and 4 respectively).

The data for the 11 representation issues were entered in a factor analysis and three logical and mathematically consistent factors emerged. Factor analysis grouped 'improving pay' and 'improving industrial benefits' (Cronbach $\alpha = 0.746$). This factor reports perceived BALPA efficacy in driving improvements in the terms and conditions of pilots' work and is thus referred to as *proactive* representation. The second factor, which includes 'legal protection' and 'support when problems arise', reflects member perception of BALPA efficacy in reacting to problems faced by flight crew and is labelled *reactive* representation (Cronbach $\alpha = 0.618$). Finally, the remaining seven issues reflect *ancillary* issues of representation (Cronbach $\alpha = 0.727$).

An OLS regression analysis was performed with the data from pilots at BA and Britannia who had experience of partnership in practice.[39] The partnership statement featured as the dependent variable; the independent variables were comprised of biographical items such as age, tenure, gender, command, etc., the efficacy statement, and the ancillary, proactive, and reactive representation factors. The results show that several variables are significantly associated with desire for partnership in practice (see Table 8.3).

Of the biographical data included, age is positively linked with desire for partnership. A descriptive analysis of these data reveals that pilots under the age of 36 were least likely to respond positively, whereas pilots over the age

*Table 8.3* OLS regression analysis (dependent: 'The Association should pursue a partnership approach with airline management')

|  | *Standardised coefficients Beta* |
| --- | --- |
| *(Constant)* | |
| Command | 0.048 |
| Tenure | −0.030 |
| Age | 0.155* |
| Gender | 0.042 |
| Gross annual salary | −0.080 |
| Efficacy statement | 0.230‡ |
| Ancillary factor | 0.158† |
| Proactive factor | 0.229‡ |
| Reactive factor | 0.089 |
| Britannia | 0.115* |

Notes
Significance levels
\* $p<0.05$.
† $p<0.01$.
‡ $p<0.001$.

*Table 8.4* Percentage of pilots in agreement with the statement 'The Association should pursue a partnership approach with airline management' (by age)

|  | *Total disagree* | *Strongly disagree* | *Disagree* | *Neither* | *Agree* | *Strongly agree* | *Total agree* |
| --- | --- | --- | --- | --- | --- | --- | --- |
| 21–35 | 32.9 | 15.8 | 17.1 | 17.1 | 36.2 | 13.8 | 50.0 |
| 36–40 | 30.3 | 12.3 | 18.0 | 7.9 | 44.9 | 16.9 | 61.8 |
| 41–45 | 28.6 | 13.0 | 15.6 | 11.7 | 40.3 | 19.4 | 59.7 |
| 46–50 | 23.0 | 16.1 | 6.9 | 17.2 | 37.8 | 21.8 | 59.8 |
| >50 | 14.8 | 6.5 | 8.3 | 12.0 | 49.1 | 24.1 | 73.2 |

of 50 were most likely to favour partnership. However, there is no consistent positive relationship between the two variables (see Table 8.4). This finding is important as it further contradicts the misconception shared by BALPA representatives and managers at BA.

Several measures of perceived BALPA efficacy correlate significantly with desire for partnership (see Table 8.2). For example, there is a positive significant relationship between efficacy and partnership. Further descriptive analysis illustrates the stark contrast between pilots at the airlines in response to the efficacy statement. A majority of pilots at Britannia agreed that BALPA was effective, while only a minority of BA pilots offered a similar assessment (see Table 8.5).

*Table 8.5* Percentage of pilots in agreement with the statement 'The Association effectively represents my interests within the airline' (by airline)

|  | Total disagree | Strongly disagree | Disagree | Neither | Agree | Strongly agree | Total agree |
|---|---|---|---|---|---|---|---|
| BA | 46.1 | 14.0 | 32.1 | 21.6 | 26.2 | 6.1 | 32.3 |
| Britannia | 20.2 | 7.3 | 12.9 | 25.0 | 42.7 | 12.1 | 54.8 |

*Table 8.6* Satisfactoriness of BALPA efficacy in improving pay (by airline)

|  | Unsatisfactory (total) | Highly un-satisfactory | Un-satisfactory | Satisfactory | Highly satisfactory | Satisfactory (total) |
|---|---|---|---|---|---|---|
| BA | 70.5 | 31.3 | 39.2 | 27.2 | 2.3 | 29.5 |
| Britannia | 37.9 | 5.6 | 32.3 | 59.7 | 2.4 | 62.1 |

*Table 8.7* Satisfactoriness of BALPA efficacy in improving industrial benefits (by airline)

|  | Unsatisfactory (total) | Highly un-satisfactory | Un-satisfactory | Satisfactory | Highly satisfactory | Satisfactory (total) |
|---|---|---|---|---|---|---|
| BA | 64.5 | 20.5 | 44.0 | 34.7 | 0.8 | 35.5 |
| Britannia | 21.0 | 1.6 | 19.4 | 68.5 | 10.5 | 79.0 |

Similarly, the ancillary and proactive representation factors are both positively and significantly linked with desire for partnership. Whereas there is a largely consistent difference in the attitudes of Britannia and BA pilots to representation issues included in the *ancillary* factor, the great contrast is between the attitudes of pilots at the two airlines in response to the issues that comprise the *proactive* factor (see Tables 8.6 and 8.7).

These data clearly support the proposition that perception of BALPA efficacy under partnership influenced desire for partnership in practice. Secondary data buttress this explanation. For example, there is evidence to suggest that the Guiding Principles partnership was blamed at least by elements of the BA flight crew community for BALPA's failure to deliver in representing their interests. In August 2001 officials at BALPA claimed that they were readying themselves for intense pay negotiations with management with a view to achieving a 'snap-back' deal for concessions made since the agreement on the Guiding Principles in 1997. In September

2001, the global civil aviation industry faced the immediate, devastating impact of the terrorist attacks on New York and Washington, after which the talks were postponed and BALPA pledged support for the survival of the airline under the ethos of partnership. A senior manager at the airline stated in late September 2001 that they had been able to achieve a great deal and 'push ahead' with their Future Size and Shape review as a result of support from the Association (*Interview notes*, September 2001).

In the election for General Secretary of BALPA in July 2002, a BA long-haul pilot, Captain John Frohnsdorff, stood as a stalking horse to challenge the incumbent General Secretary and pioneer of the Guiding Principles partnership, Chris Darke. Disgruntled by the moderate approach taken by BALPA in negotiations with the airline, Captain Frohnsdorff detailed three issues in his manifesto for election, including an explicit promise to end the partnership, which he claimed was a widespread source of disaffection:

> Our industry terms and conditions have slipped steadily by inter-national standards and there is a widespread feeling that the 'Guiding Principles' (a partnership approach with management) championed by the General Secretary, has exacerbated this decline, with BA for instance held to little if any accountability for repeated transgressions. What other airlines have similar appeasements?
>
> (quoted from Captain John Frohnsdorff's election manifesto, www.pprune.com)

Darke was defeated by a margin of 2 votes to 1. The anonymous ballot makes it impossible to analyse voting patterns and show whether those voting against him were predominantly employed at BA.

In contrast, at Britannia management was considerably better placed than BA to accede to union demands after September 11, the consequent economic circumstances of both airlines varying enormously. At Britannia, profit for the year ending December 2001 was £61 million, nearly double that of the previous year. BA, undoubtedly the UK airline to suffer most, posted losses of around £200 million, its greatest since privatisation. Compared with negotiations at BA, BALPA negotiations with manage-ment at Britannia are more likely to have delivered successful results for flight crew in the aftermath of the crisis and the period immediately before the distribution of the questionnaire survey, thereby enhancing members' views of BALPA efficacy, and consequently the efficacy of partnership.

It should be noted that these data are cross-sectional and therefore it is impossible to be certain about the direction of causality. Due to the nature of the data, then, it is not possible to conclusively demonstrate that perception of BALPA efficacy leads to desire for partnership, as interpreted above. It is reasonable to assume that pilots are generally not fundamentally opposed to partnership, as demonstrated by the widespread advocacy of partnership in principle at the low-cost airlines, Air2000 and bmi, and the similarly extensive agreement with partnership in practice at Britannia. The desire for partnership, or comparative lack thereof, among BA pilots must be the result of a post hoc evaluation of partnership in practice.

It is possible, however, that the lack of desire for partnership among pilots at the British flag carrier was not the result of an instrumental assessment of BALPA efficacy in representing the interests of pilots under partnership. Attitudes may have been influenced by dissatisfaction with the nature of the new relationship between the Association and management, and the resultant closeness of the union to management. From this perspective it might feasibly be argued that pilots who were opposed to the consequent convivial bond between union and management had registered their complaint by offering a negative evaluation of union efficacy. Therefore, consistent with the concerns expressed by union members in previous studies of partnership, desire for partnership among pilots, and indeed their evaluation of BALPA efficacy, could have been a function of discontent with the perceived incorporation of the Association into management, and the lack of BALPA autonomy under the new arrangement.

Both of these interpretations of the data are consistent with the explanation that perceived union effectiveness under partnership determines desire for partnership in practice. After all, Hyman[40] presents three pillars of union effectiveness: autonomy, legitimacy, and efficacy. The first interpretation of the data links desire for partnership with the perception of union efficacy under partnership, while the second links desire for partnership with the perception of union legitimacy and autonomy under partnership. Either way, these data confirm that the union must remain effective in the eyes of the membership for partnership to be desirable in practice.

## Conclusion

Chapter 7 revealed that HRM style and membership commitment to the union were positively and significantly associated. That is, where management has pursued a high degree of collectivism and individualism in HRM style, pilots were more likely to be committed to the union. The ostensible implications of this finding are that the union stands to benefit from co-operative collectivism in HRM style and should engage management in partnership as the optimum approach that will yield membership approval.

This chapter has explored the response of pilots to partnership as an expression of cooperation between union and management. The data clearly demonstrate that partnership in principle was widely seen as desirable: that this approach was congruent with the image the pilots wish to convey of themselves and their Association, as professionals and a professional association respectively. The data also exhibit a large variation in response between the two airlines where pilots have experience of partnership in practice. The airlines differ considerably in size. However, it was impossible to test the proposition that size matters in terms of attitudes towards partnership among flight crew. Speculation among airline management and BALPA representatives that attitudes towards partnership were a function of pilot tenure proved inconsistent with the data. An alternative explanation focused on perceived union effectiveness under partnership as the key variable in determining desire for partnership. To assess this proposition, analysis was conducted and a significant positive association was found between evaluation of BALPA efficacy and desire for partnership.

The attitudes of rank-and-file members towards partnership are critical to its success and potentially to the survival of the union. For pilots, partnership in principle is consistent with the image pilots wish to convey and, arguably, is widely desired as a result. However, it will only receive similar approval in practice if the union is seen by the membership to be effective while engaging in partnership: remaining autonomous, retaining its legitimacy, and maintaining its efficacy.

# 9    Conclusion

## Introduction

People management in the airline industry is extremely important. Reducing operational costs has become a major preoccupation of airline management and employees represent the single largest flexible cost to an airline.[1] Consequently, airline management has both the motive and the opportunity[2] to reduce labour costs. However, civil aviation is fundamentally a service industry, where employees can make a considerable difference to customer choice. Moreover, employees can halt airline activity through industrial action, so ensuring they are satisfied and enhancing organisational commitment among them must be a primary objective of management.

Flight crew pose airline management a particular problem because they are non-substitutable and well organised and therefore can impose severe sanctions on the airline. They are also, increasingly, among the most valuable commodities in airline operations (which cannot do without them), because of the rising demand for air transport and the anticipated scarcity of flight crew. In other words, airline management must prevent pilot *exit* and assuage antagonistic demonstrations of pilot *voice*, as both can be highly damaging to the airline. Prior research has shown that employees who report job satisfaction and organisational commitment are more likely to show discretionary effort and less likely either to participate in industrial action or to leave the firm.

With some evidence of outcomes such as increased job satisfaction and organisational commitment, HRM promises a panacea for the people management dilemma faced by airline management. However, despite almost 30 years of debate, the concept of HRM remains somewhat ambiguous and the findings of research into its effect on firm performance and employee attitudes are far from conclusive. A necessary first step was to define HRM. Following a recent trend in the debate,[3] two components of HRM were identified. The first is the content of HRM, which refers to the policies and practices implemented by management concerning recruitment and selection and reward management, for example. Content is most regularly the focus of HRM studies. Second, there is HRM style, derived from Purcell's concept of 'management style',[4] including individual and collective dimensions. Like its preceding component of management style, individualism in HRM style is expressed in the 'extent to which the firm gives credence to the feelings and sentiments of each employee and seeks to develop and encourage each employee's capacity and role at work'.[5] For flight crew this includes promoting the professionalism of pilots, emphasising their technical contribution, respecting their professional status, and providing stable work organisation. It is distinct from Purcell's conception of individualism in management style, as the comparable dimension of HRM style is not evidenced in HRM content implemented by management. Collectivism in HRM style concerns the manner in which airline management negotiates with BALPA, but unlike the comparable dimension of management style, it is demonstrated by engagement with independent collective representatives rather than in-house methods of collective representation.

The study of management in the airline industry assessed the impact of these distinct components of HRM on the attitudes of flight crew. In essence, this study addressed three research questions with data from six airlines that adequately represent the three principal market sub-sectors of the UK civil aviation industry, i.e. full service, low cost, and charter. The analysis incorporated secondary data from trade journals, newspapers, the CAA, and the airlines themselves, and primary data from managers at several of the airlines, BALPA officials and BALPA pilot representatives, and unionised pilots at the six airlines. Primary data collection techniques included interviews, focus groups, and a large-scale questionnaire survey. These data addressed the following questions.

## Do UK airlines converge on HRM in the management of pilots?

It is generally accepted that HRM enhances firm performance through HRM policies and practices that encourage employees to improve and utilise their skills and abilities.[6] HRM policies and practices are imitable, however.[7] Due to the vital importance of competent people management in airlines, and with forces for isomorphism[8] abounding in the civil aviation industry, one might expect management to adopt similar 'best practices' in the management of labour across the industry. The facet of HRM labelled style in this book has not inspired a similar level of interest and thus airlines are less likely to converge on a single model. Indeed, research conducted in the US[9] identifies several different styles. Convergence on both HRM content and style was assessed in this book.

Prior research reveals a dissonance of perception between management and employee of the presence of HRM.[10] Measurement error has also been identified in single respondent management data.[11] Consequently, the content and style of HRM at the six airlines were assessed on the basis of secondary source data, with primary data from flight crew rather than management (although in two cases, data from flight crew were augmented with data from management). As part of a large-scale survey of pilots, respondents were presented with a list of 26 policies and practices associated with HRM,[12] and asked to identify which had been implemented at their airlines in the management of flight crew.

Each of the 26 policies and practices were identified at the six airlines, albeit the extent of recognition varied between airlines. This illustrates convergence on HRM content among UK airlines. Given that pilots at all six airlines identified each of the policies and practices, it seems that the HRM 'tables stakes'[13] for managing pilots are especially high. However, the response of pilots at several airlines (for example, at bmi and Air2000) revealed a particularly limited acknowledgement of the policies and practices. Clearly, the process of HRM implementation has been less effective in these airlines than it has in other airlines (for example, Go and Britannia). In other words, the stakes are high, and inevitably some play the game much better than others.

There are, however, two distinctive models of HRM style apparent. HRM style at the low-cost airline, Go, and the charter airline, Britannia, emphasises the professional status of flight crew (high individualism) and favours a cooperative approach towards BALPA (cooperative collectivism). In contrast, HRM style at the low-cost airline, easyJet, at the charter airline, Air2000, and at the full-service airline, bmi, devalues the status of flight crew (low individualism) and relies on an adversarial collectivism. Thus, in contrast to HRM content, and in spite of considerable isomorphic pressure, airlines have pursued diverse HRM styles, reminiscent of management in the US airline industry. This finding implies that the claim made by Warhurst[14] – that there has been convergence in HRM among European airlines – is too sweeping.

## What is the impact of HRM on the attitudes of flight crew?

Increased job satisfaction and enhanced organisational commitment are perennially identified as outcomes of HRM by advocates and so the study analysed the impact of HRM on these attitudes among flight crew. The data reveal no consistent association between the presence of HRM content and either job satisfaction or organisational commitment. However, a powerful and positive relationship between HRM style and both job satisfaction and organisational commitment was identified, with satisfaction and commitment more likely among pilots at airlines where management were committed to a high degree of individualism and co-operative collectivism in HRM style.

The findings also contribute to the debate concerning 'best fit' and 'best practice'. The data confirm that the operational strategy of the airline does not and indeed should not determine the style of its HRM for it to max-imise its advantage through its people. At the low-cost airline, Go, man-agement pursued a style more closely aligned with a high-quality operational strategy, emphasising the professionalism of flight crew and seeking a closer working relationship with BALPA. Pilots at the airline were among the most satisfied with their work and committed to the success of the airline, which enjoyed enviable profitability. At easyJet, itself a highly successful low-cost airline in which the HRM style was more consistent with the operational strategy (de-emphasising the profes-sionalism of flight crew and opposing BALPA involvement), pilots were the least likely to report satisfaction with work and were among the least committed to the success of the airline. As stated above, the attitudes of flight crew are of paramount import as expressions of discontent can cause the airline tremendous difficulties. The narrow avoidance of the threat of industrial action by pilots at easyJet in 2004 resulted in an alternative management strategy towards BALPA. In 2005, airline management sought a closer working relationship with the Association, exemplified by collaboration between union and management in the design of a new roster system for flight crew (*Interview notes*, October 2005). In terms of HRM style, airlines would do well to adopt the 'best practice' of high indi-vidualism and cooperative collectivism.

A theme in the organisational commitment literature examines the rela-tionship between commitment to the organisation and commitment to the union. It has been argued that the greatest threat HRM poses to trade union-ism occurs through its impact on organisational commitment, because an employee committed to the organisation is for that very reason less likely to become involved in union activity. The data indicate that union commit-ment is significantly and positively associated with organisational commit-ment and hence, for pilots, not only were the two compatible but there was a greater likelihood of finding commitment to both parties than commit-ment to neither or univocal commitment to either the organisation or the union. The implication that the union stands to benefit in terms of member-ship commitment by engaging with airline management in partnership, in a joint expression of high collectivism, was also explored.

## Do pilots desire partnership?

The implications of partnership for the strategic position of the trade union, and of partnership on outcomes for members in terms of wages, employment levels, and the like, are important research questions.[15] The impact of partnership on the attitudes of members towards the trade union has not generated comparable data, yet is central to the debate.[16] Recent studies have illustrated a negative response on the part of union members to partnership.[17] There are several reasons why one might anticipate a more positive response to partnership from pilots. First, partnership is consistent with the professional image pilots wish to convey of themselves and of their union. Second, pilots stand to gain more from partnership than other employee groups, being highly trained and educated, and thereby better able to take advantage of a greater involvement and participation in the workplace.

The data reveal widespread desire for partnership in principle among pilots at the airlines where BALPA had not agreed a partnership at the time of the study. However, there was a significant difference in the attitudes of pilots at the two partnership airlines. Desire for partnership in practice among pilots with experience of such a relationship was powerfully associated with their perception of union efficacy. At BA, pilots were significantly less likely to desire partnership in practice or to evaluate BALPA positively than their counterparts at Britannia. It is clear that desire for partnership in practice was powerfully influenced by the pilot's perception of BALPA effectiveness under partnership.

## Implications for airline management and BALPA

The findings of this study have policy implications for BALPA and for airline management. Partnership in principle was widely popular among flight crew, but the Association should be aware that attitudes towards partnership in practice were very much dependent upon the perception of union effectiveness under partnership. The election defeat of former General Secretary of BALPA Chris Darke can be attributed to some degree to the level of dissatisfaction with partnership among BA pilots, one of whom challenged him for his post. It is clear that BALPA policy should be informed by the attitudes of its members. The data show that organisational commitment and commitment to the union are not mutually exclusive. Indeed, commitment to both the organisation and the union was more likely than commitment to either separately. Therefore, the Association appears to gain from cooperative collectivism in HRM style. That said, the analysis in Chapter 8 illustrates the potential dangers of union acquiescence to a joint policy of cooperation with management, through partnership for example. Unless the union remains effective in the eyes of its members under partnership, then the approach can be problematic. Whereas it might be argued that dissatisfaction with partnership led to a resurgence of unionism among BA pilots, rather than the demobilisation predicted by Kelly,[18] there is good reason to believe that a less positive outcome would result from such discontent among flight crew in other airlines.

At the time of study, the BA flight crew community provided the mainstay of BALPA membership, with some 3000 members comprising approximately 85 per cent of the BA pilot community. The relationship between BALPA and BA, formerly BOAC and BEA, is steeped in history and remains so strong that the abbreviation BALPA is often misconstrued as the *British Airways* Line Pilots Association. It is therefore reasonable to assume that BA pilots have the greatest incentive to ensure the institution survives. As no such tradition exists for pilots of other airlines, we might expect no such desire for BALPA to prevail. We can only speculate what might be the consequence of dissatisfaction with the association among flight crew who have less investment in the survival of BALPA.

There is clearly a necessity for management to ensure that pilots are satisfied in their work and committed to their airline. The data reveal that organisational commitment and job satisfaction are significantly linked to the HRM style adopted by airline management. For airline management, then, the data provide a powerful argument in favour of both negotiating in good faith and involving the Association more fully in the decision-making processes of the airline, and for acknowledging the professional and technical significance of flight crew and ensuring stability in work schedules. In other words, the data present a business case for pursuing a high degree of individualism and cooperative collectivism in HRM style. Management should also be aware that investment in costly HRM policies and practices (content) may be undermined by pursuing an antagonistic approach with pilots as individuals and as a collective. Thus, it is essential that management not only play the game with comparable table stakes (HRM content) but also raise their game to the appropriate style.

# Notes

## 1  Introduction

1  Blain (1972).
2  Freeman and Medoff (1984); Hirschmann (1970).
3  Harvey (2001); Turnbull *et al.* (2004).
4  Doganis (2006: 128).
5  Warhurst (1995).
6  Kaufman (2003); Swiercz and Spencer (1992).
7  Bruch and Sattelberger (2001).
8  Pfeffer (1997).
9  Gittell (2003); Pfeffer (1994).
10  Wood (1999).
11  Grant and Shields (2002).
12  Purcell *et al.* (2003).
13  See, for example, Ramsay *et al.* (2000).
14  Ramsay *et al.* (2000).
15  Bowey and Thorpe (1986); Purcell *et al.* (2003).
16  Schuler (1992).
17  Schuler (1992: 21).
18  Pfeffer (1994: 58–59).
19  Boxall and Purcell (2003: 69).
20  Purcell (1981).
21  Purcell (1987).
22  Purcell *et al.* (2003).
23  Boxall and Purcell (2003: 69).
24  Edwards and Wright (2001).
25  Guest (2005).
26  See Kelly (2004).
27  DiMaggio and Powell (1983).
28  Purcell (1999).

## 2  Civil aviation and the airline pilot

1  Boxall (2003: 5).
2  Korczynski (2002: 1).
3  Harvey and Turnbull (2002: 1).

## 132   *Notes*

4  Roberto Gonzalez, keynote address to the World Civil Aviation Chief Executives, 26 December 2006.
5  C.G. Grey quoted in Blain (1972: 63).
6  It should be noted that Simon Bennett's (2006) *A Sociology of Commercial Flight Crew* considers many work-related issues and collects data from pilots from around the globe, including UK-based pilots.
7  Quoted by Rigby (1997).
8  Bennett (2006: 64).
9  Quoted by Pilling and Field (2003).
10  Blyton *et al.* (1998b); Turnbull and Harvey (2001); Doganis (2006: 136–137).
11  Blyton *et al.* (1998a).
12  Wright (2000).
13  Wright (2000: 962).
14  Ionides *et al.* (2007).
15  Granistas and Westlake (2001); Hearn (2006); McCartney (2000); Moorman (2000); Thomas (2005).
16  'BA "excludes mothers as pilots"', http://news.bbc.co.uk/1/hi/uk/4160447.stm (accessed 13 March 2007).
17  Johnson (2002: 22).
18  'How to become a commercial pilot', www.BALPA.org.uk
19  'How to become a commercial pilot', www.BALPA.org.uk
20  Eaton (2001: 100).
21  Blyton *et al.* (1999); Grugulis and Wilkinson (2002).
22  News in brief, 'BMI pilots vote for strike', *Travel Weekly* (1 September 2006), p. 5.
23  News in brief, 'BA pilots threaten pension strike', *Travel Weekly* (3 March 2006), p. 3.
24  Bennett (2006: 67).
25  Wolmar (1996).
26  Blain (1972).
27  Johnson (2002: 38).
28  Cappelli (1985: 332).
29  Freeman and Medoff (1984); Hirschman (1970).
30  'Upheaval in the European skies', a report by ECA (2002).
31  QRN (questionnaire respondent number) is the number attributed to the questionnaire survey as its data were inputted. This number does not reflect the order in which the questionnaires were received.
32  Bennett (2006: 75–80).
33  See Harvey and Turnbull (2002: 7–9).
34  Watkins (2003: 12).
35  Doganis (2006: 141).
36  Doganis (2006: 122).
37  Doganis (2006: 121).
38  Based on statistics from 2002 (see Doganis 2006: 121).
39  Based on the average pilot salaries presented by Doganis (2006: 121).
40  Doganis (2006: 118).
41  Doganis (2006: 24); see also Blyton *et al.* (1998a).
42  Blyton *et al.* (1998a: 3).
43  Industry review, 'Rebel skies: the history', *Flight International*, 9 April 2002.

*Notes* 133

44  Blyton *et al.* (1998b: 7).
45  Blyton *et al.* (1998b: 7).
46  Doganis (2006: 76).
47  Doganis (2006: 85).
48  Blyton *et al.* (1999: 8).
49  Industry review, 'Rebel skies: the history', *Flight International*, 9 April 2002.
50  Industry review, 'Rebel skies: the market', *Flight International*, 9 April 2002.
51  ECA (2002: 7).
52  Saunders (2002: 48).
53  Saunders (2002: 48).
54  ECA (2002: 5).
55  ECA (2002: 5).
56  ECA (2002: 5).
57  ECA (2002: 19).
58  Bennett (2003: 207).
59  See Harvey and Turnbull (2002).
60  Colling (1995: 24).
61  Boyd (1999: 446).
62  Doganis (2006: 137–138).
63  Doganis (2001: 118); see also Doganis (2006: 139–140).
64  Blyton *et al.* (1998b: 15); Blyton *et al.* (1999: 8).
65  Doganis (2001: 119).
66  Blyton *et al.* (1998b: 17).
67  Blyton *et al.* (1999: 11).
68  See Blyton *et al.* (1998a).
69  Blyton *et al.* (1998a: 5).
70  Blyton *et al.* (1998a: 6).
71  Blyton *et al.* (1998a: 8).
72  Blyton *et al.* (1998a: 7–8).
73  Blyton *et al.* (1998a: 9–10).
74  Blyton *et al.* (1998a: 9–10).
75  Blyton *et al.* (1998a: 13).
76  Quoted in Harvey and Turnbull (2002: 2).
77  Coulter (2002: 26).
78  Coulter (2002: 26).
79  Turnbull and Harvey (2001).
80  Blyton *et al.* (1998a: 3).

## 3  The content and style of human resource management

1  Keenoy (1999).
2  Blyton and Turnbull (1992: 2).
3  Fombrun *et al.* (1984).
4  Beer *et al.* (1984).
5  Schuler and Jackson (1987).
6  Hendry *et al.* (1989).
7  Purcell *et al.* (2003).
8  Kinnie *et al.* (2006).
9  Boxall (1996, 1998).
10  Huselid (1995).

11  Patterson *et al.* (1997).
12  Penrose (1959).
13  Barney (1991).
14  Penrose (1959: 31).
15  Barney (1991: 101).
16  Barney (1991: 105–106).
17  Wright *et al.* (1994).
18  Wright *et al.* (1994: 318).
19  Kinnie *et al.* (2006: 41).
20  Levitt and Dubner (2005).
21  Parker and Slaughter (1988).
22  See Whitener (2001).
23  Bratton and Gold (2003: 413–415), although it should be noted that the authors list four challenges to trade unionism.
24  Bratton and Gold (2003: 414).
25  Legge (1995: 272).
26  Hoell (2004: 274).
27  Kelly (1998: 61–64). Kelly refers to the 'anti-union logic of human resource management' (1998: 62).
28  Kelly (1998: 61).
29  Kelly (1998: 61).
30  Guest and Hoque (1996); Millward (1994).
31  Kelly (1998: 22, emphasis in original).
32  Guest (2005; 2001).
33  Guest (2005: 239–40).
34  Storey (1992); Cully *et al.* (1999).
35  Guest (1995); Guest and Conway (1999).
36  Guest (2001: 97).
37  Boxall and Purcell (2003: 1); Sisson (1990: 1); Poole (1990: 1).
38  Boxall and Purcell (2003: 179–182).
39  Purcell (1987).
40  Purcell (1987: 535).
41  Purcell (1987: 536).
42  Purcell (1987: 536).
43  Purcell (1987: 538).
44  Purcell (1987: 539).
45  Purcell (1987: 538).
46  Purcell (1987: 539).
47  Purcell (1987: 541).
48  Purcell (1987: 540).
49  Purcell (1987: 539).
50  Bacon and Storey (1993: 9–10).
51  See Gittell *et al.* (2004).
52  See Purcell (1999); Legge (2001); Edwards and Wright (2001); Delaney and Godard (2001) and Godard (2001).
53  Purcell (1999).
54  Legge (2001: 30).
55  Delaney and Godard (2001: 408).
56  Godard (2001: 799).
57  Legge (2001).

58  See Delaney and Godard (2001); Guest (1999); Gardener *et al.* (2001); Legge (2001); Ramsay *et al.* (2000).
59  See Gardener *et al.* (2001: 32, emphasis added).
60  See Sano (1998).
61  Harrison *et al.* (2006).
62  Guest (1999).
63  Ramsay *et al.* (2000).
64  Truss (2001: 1141).
65  Wright *et al.* (2001: 893).
66  Wright and Boswell (2002: 263–264); see also Deery (2002).
67  Meyer and Smith (2000).
68  Meyer and Smith (2000: 320).
69  See Delbridge and Turnbull (1992).
70  A term coined by Eisenberger *et al.* (1986).
71  Wayne *et al.* (1997).
72  Eisenberger *et al.* (1986: 501).
73  Boxall and Purcell (2003: 69) discuss HRM in terms of surface and underpinning layers.
74  Guest (2005: 245).
75  Sisson (1993: 206); Cully *et al.* (1999: 111).
76  Cully *et al.* (1999: 135).
77  Baird and Meshoulam (1988).
78  Pfeffer (1994; 1998).
79  See, for example, Pudelko (2005); Sparrow *et al.* (1994); Tregaskis and Brewster (2006).
80  DiMaggio and Powell (1983).
81  Child (1972).
82  Aldrich (1979).
83  DiMaggio and Powell (1983: 147).
84  Colling (1995); Warhurst (1995); Blyton and Turnbull (1996).
85  Gittell *et al.* (2004).
86  Gittell *et al.* (2004: 169).
87  Gittell *et al.* (2004: 169).
88  Gittell *et al.* (2004: 169–171).
89  Kochan *et al.* (1987: 35).
90  Guest (1995: 137).
91  Bacon and Storey (1993).
92  See Blyton and Turnbull (2004: chapter 5).
93  Ackers and Payne (1998: 530).
94  Ackers and Payne (1998: 530).
95  Ackers and Payne (1998: 531).
96  Ackers and Payne (1998: 533).
97  Ackers and Payne (1998: 533).
98  Ackers and Payne (1998: 547).
99  Oxenbridge and Brown (2002).
100  Oxenbridge and Brown (2002: 273).
101  Oxenbridge and Brown (2002: 273).
102  Kelly (1998: 63).
103  Bacon and Storey (2000).
104  Bacon and Storey (2000: 424).

## 4  The research project: a methodology

1  Britannia Airways has been renamed Thomsonfly since the study.
2  Air2000 has been renamed First Choice Airways.
3  Gill and Johnson (1997: 157).
4  See Sull (1999); Blyton and Turnbull (2004); Hopfl *et al.* (1992); Colling (1995); Turnbull *et al.* (2004).
5  Cassani and Kemp (2003).
6  Johnson and Duberley (2003).
7  Spencer (1983).
8  Blain (1972: 28).
9  As suggested by Oppenheim (1992: 67).
10  As proposed by Denzin (1970: 297).
11  Merton *et al.* (1956).
12  Fontana and Frey (1994: 365).
13  Gill and Johnson (1997: 81).
14  Namely, Wood and Albanese (1995); Ramsay *et al.* (2000); and Guest (1999).
15  Flin and Martin (2001: 96).
16  Hedge *et al.* (2000: 378).
17  Wright *et al.* (1994).
18  Flin and Martin (2001: 96).
19  Flin and Martin (2001: 111).
20  Hedge *et al.* (2000); Flin and Martin (2001).
21  Flin and Martin (2001: 103).
22  Blain (1972).
23  Fowler (2002: 16).
24  See Fowler (2002); and Frankfort-Nachmias and Nachmias (1996: 227) for a general discussion of the impact of the perceived legitimacy of the research on the response rate.
25  Frankfort-Nachmias and Nachmias (1996: 228).
26  Frankfort-Nachmias and Nachmias (1996: 228).
27  Fowler (2002: 48).

## 5  The content and style of HRM in UK airlines

1  Purcell (1987).
2  Purcell (1987: 536).
3  Bacon (2001: 369); see also Marchington and Grugulis (2000).
4  Gittell *et al.* (2004).
5  Wright *et al.* (2001); Wright and Boswell (2002).
6  See Pollock (2001).
7  See Bacon (1999); Cully *et al.* (1999); Grant and Shields (2002).
8  Hoque (2003: 565).
9  Purcell (1999: 36).
10  Professional status was an issue of utmost concern for UK flight crew in Blain's (1972) study.
11  Sull (1999).
12  Sull (1999: 25).
13  Quoted in Sull (1999: 25).

14  Quoted in Sull (1999: 23).
15  Pollock (2001).
16  Pollock (2001: 50).
17  Pollock (2001: 50).
18  Purcell (1987: 537).
19  Purcell (1987).
20  Cassani and Kemp (2003: 94).
21  Korczynski (2002: 15).
22  Cassani and Kemp (2003: 90).
23  Cassani and Kemp (2003: 102).
24  Cassani and Kemp (2003: 51).
25  Cassani and Kemp (2003: 44).
26  Cassani and Kemp (2003: 44).
27  Cassani and Kemp (2003: 102).
28  Cassani and Kemp (2003: 102).
29  Cassani and Kemp (2003: 103).
30  Cassani and Kemp (2003: 43).
31  Cassani and Kemp (2003: 132).
32  Cassani and Kemp (2003: 133).
33  Von Nordenflycht (2002).
34  Kochan *et al.* (2003).
35  See, for example, Colling (1995); Harvey (2001); Hopfl *et al.* (1992); Turnbull *et al.* (2004); Warhurst (1995).
36  See Blyton and Turnbull (2004: chapter 4).
37  See Blyton *et al.* (2001); Blyton and Turnbull (2004); Grugulis and Wilkinson (2002); and Turnbull *et al.* (2004).
38  BA General Manager quoted in Harvey (2001).
39  Harvey (2001); Turnbull *et al.* (2004).
40  See Harvey (2001); Blyton and Turnbull (2004); Turnbull *et al.* (2004).
41  Doganis (2006: 121).
42  'EasyJet/Go merge, bmibaby grows up', *Flight International*, 6 August 2002.
43  Harrison (2002).
44  Anonymity requested by interviewee.
45  Anonymity requested by interviewee.
46  'TUI Low Cost Launch', *Airline Business*, 1 January 2004.
47  Phillips (2003).
48  'Britannia and TCUK Eye Wireless Systems', *Flight International*, 8 July 2003.
49  Hope (2002).
50  Pilling (2003).
51  Pilling (2003).
52  Turnbull *et al.* (2004).
53  Baker (2003).
54  Pilling (2001).
55  Scheerhoot (2003).
56  'Clouds Continue to Gather at First Choice', *Evening Standard*, 30 August 1996.
57  'Your All Singing, All Dancing Crew', *The Times*, 25 October 2003; news in brief, 'Be Human, Witty, Sexy', *Travel Trade Gazette UK & Ireland*, 13 October 2003, p. 8.

## 6   HRM and job satisfaction

1   Locke (1976: 1300).
2   Freeman (1978: 135).
3   Freeman (1978: 138).
4   Akerlof *et al.* (1988).
5   McEvoy and Cascio (1985).
6   Clark (1996: 189).
7   Shields and Ward (2001).
8   Scott *et al.* (2006).
9   Clark (1996: 197).
10   Clark (1996: 198).
11   Bender and Heywood (2006: 254).
12   Clark (1996: 202).
13   Clark (1996: 201).
14   Clark (1996: 203).
15   Idson (1990).
16   Idson (1990: 1016).
17   Clark (1996: 193); see also Gazioglu and Tansel (2006).
18   Scott *et al.* (2006).
19   Idson (1990).
20   Clark (1996).
21   Gazioglu and Tansel (2006).
22   Clark (1996); Gazioglu and Tansel (2006).
23   Clark (1996).
24   QRN (questionnaire respondent number) is the number attributed to the questionnaire survey as its data were inputted. This number does not reflect the order in which the questionnaires were returned.
25   Herrbach and Mignonac (2004).
26   See Harvey and Turnbull (2002).
27   Doganis (2006: 121).

## 7   HRM, organisational commitment, and commitment to the union

1   NB I argue here that pilots committed to the organisation are less likely to become involved in industrial action, not that pilots committed to the organisation are less likely to be committed to their union.
2   Guest (2005: 239–240).
3   See Beer *et al.* (1984); Guest (1987).
4   Purcell *et al.* (2003).
5   Slocombe and Dougherty (1998: 469).
6   See Swailes (2004: 188).
7   Meyer and Allen (1991: 67).
8   See Slocombe and Dougherty (1998: 470); Swailes (2004: 188); Johnson and Chang (2006: 550); Herrbach (2006: 631); Payne and Huffman (2005: 159).
9   Zhou and George (2001: 682).
10   Zhou and George (2001: 682).
11   Meyer and Smith (2000: 320).
12   Culpepper *et al.* (2004: 157).

13 Culpepper *et al.* (2004).
14 See Iverson and Buttigieg (1999); Clugston (2000); Payne and Huffman (2005).
15 Gallie *et al.* (2001: 1085).
16 Legge (1995: 182).
17 See Gallie *et al.* (2001: 1082).
18 Gallie *et al.* (2001: 1094).
19 Bryson (2004: 213).
20 Meyer and Smith (2000).
21 Meyer and Smith (2000: 319).
22 Kinicki *et al.* (1992).
23 Koys (1988; 1991).
24 See Meyer and Smith (2000: 320).
25 Meyer and Smith (2000: 329).
26 Purcell (1987: 536).
27 Guest (2005: 245).
28 Bryson (2001: 102).
29 Guest and Conway (1999: 375).
30 See Porter *et al.* (1974); Cook and Wall (1980).
31 Gallie *et al.* (2001: 1086).
32 Gallie *et al.* (2001: 1094).
33 QRN (questionnaire respondent number) is the number attributed to the questionnaire survey as its data were inputted. This number does not reflect the order in which the questionnaires were returned.
34 Adams (1965).
35 Wallace (1995: 246).
36 Guest (1989).
37 Guest (2005: 239–240).
38 Angle and Perry (1986); Carson *et al.* (2006); Dean (1954); Murphy and Olthuis (1995); Purcell (1954).
39 Carson *et al.* (2006: 138).
40 Angle and Perry (1986).
41 Carson *et al.* (2006: 138).
42 Magenau *et al.* (1988).
43 Carson *et al.* (2006).
44 Dean (1954); Purcell (1954).
45 Hoell (2004: 269).
46 Guest and Dewe (1991).
47 Deery *et al.* (1994).
48 Deery *et al.* (1994: 593).
49 Angle and Perry (1986: 49).
50 Gordon *et al.* (1980).
51 Deery *et al.* (1994).

## 8 Pilots and partnership

1 Hyman (1975).
2 See Kelly (2004) and Masters *et al.* (2006).
3 Roche and Geary (2002).
4 Ackers and Payne (1998).
5 Ackers and Payne (1998: 533).

6  Ackers and Payne (1998: 547).
7  Kochan and Osterman (1994: 217–218).
8  Kochan and Osterman (1994: 219).
9  Kochan and Osterman (1994: 220).
10  Kelly (1996; 1998).
11  Wright (2000: 971).
12  Hyman (1971: 19).
13  Hyman (1971: 17).
14  Hyman (1971: 19).
15  Marks *et al.* (1998).
16  Marks *et al.* (1998: 220–222).
17  Marks *et al.* (1998: 222).
18  Johnstone *et al.* (2004: 367).
19  Danford *et al.* (2005).
20  Danford *et al.* (2005: 188).
21  Wright (2000).
22  Johnson (2002: 22).
23  See Blyton *et al.* (1999) and Grugulis and Wilkinson (2002).
24  ECA (2002).
25  Kelly (2004).
26  Turnbull *et al.* (2004: 290).
27  Blyton and Turnbull (2004: 261–262).
28  Blain (1972).
29  Kochan and Osterman (1994).
30  See Turnbull *et al.* (2004).
31  Pilling (2003).
32  Pilling (2003).
33  Pilling (2003).
34  Oxenbridge and Brown (2002).
35  Output in available tonne kilometre (ATK) is a common measure of the scale of an airline's operation.
36  Child (1988).
37  Mintzberg (1979).
38  See Wright (2000).
39  The application of parametric tests to non-parametric data is discussed in Chapter 7 and Chapter 4.
40  Hyman (1975).

## 9  Conclusion

1  Doganis (2006: 118).
2  Blyton *et al.* (1999).
3  See Boxall and Purcell (2003); Purcell *et al.* (2003).
4  Purcell (1987).
5  Purcell (1987: 536).
6  See, for example, Gardener *et al.* (2001); Guest (1999); Patterson *et al.* (1997); Purcell *et al.* (2003); Wright *et al.* (1994).
7  Bacon (2001); Marchington and Grugulis (2000).
8  DiMaggio and Powell (1983).
9  Gittell *et al.* (2004).

10  See, for example, Cully *et al.* (1999); Bacon (1999).
11  Wright *et al.* (2001).
12  As identified by Guest (1999); Ramsay *et al.* (2000); and Wood and Albanese (1995).
13  Purcell (1999).
14  Warhurst (1995).
15  For example, Bacon and Storey (2000); Cutcher-Gershenfeld and Kochan (2004); Deery and Iverson (2005); Guest and Peccei (2001); Kelly (2004); Kochan *et al.* (1986); Masters *et al.* (2006); Oxenbridge and Brown (2002; 2004).
16  Kelly (1996; 1998; 1999); Roche and Geary (2002).
17  For example, Johnstone *et al.* (2004); Roche and Geary (2002); Danford *et al.* (2004).
18  Kelly (1998).

# References

Ackers, P. and Payne, J. (1998) 'British trade unions and social partnership: rhetoric, reality and strategy', *International Journal of Human Resource Management*, 9(3), pp. 529–550.

Adams, J.S. (1965) 'Injustice in social exchange', in Berkowitz, L. (ed.) *Advances in Experimental Psychology*, New York: Academic Press.

Akerlof, G.A., Rose, A.K., and Yellen, J.L. (1988) 'Job switching and job satisfaction in the US labor market', *Brookings Papers on Economic Activity*, 2, pp. 495–582.

Aldrich, H. (1979) *Organizations and Their Environments*, New Jersey: Prentice Hall.

Angle, H.L. and Perry, J.L. (1986) 'Dual commitment and labor–management relationship climates', *Academy of Management Journal*, 29(1), pp. 31–50.

Bacon, N. (1999) 'The realities of human resource management?', *Human Relations*, 52(9), pp. 1179–1187.

Bacon, N. (2001) 'Competitive advantage through human resource management: best practices or core competencies?', *Human Relations*, 54(3), pp. 361–372.

Bacon, N. and Storey, J. (1993) 'Individualization of the employment relationship and the implications for trade unions', *Employee Relations*, 15(1), pp. 5–17.

Bacon, N. and Storey, J. (2000) 'New employee relations strategies in Britain: towards individualism or partnership?', *British Journal of Industrial Relations*, 38(3), pp. 407–427.

Baird, L. and Meshoulam, I. (1988) 'Managing two fits of strategic human resource management', *Academy of Management Review*, 13(1), pp. 116–128.

Baker, C. (2003) 'Travel troubles', *Airline Business*, 19(10), October, pp. 68–71.

Barney, J. (1991) 'Firm resources and sustained competitive advantage', *Journal of Management*, 17(1), pp. 99–120.

Beer, M., Spector, B., Lawrence, P.R., Quinn Mills, D., and Walton, R.E. (1984) *Managing Human Assets*, New York: Free Press.

Bender, K.A. and Heywood, J.S. (2006) 'Job satisfaction of the highly educated: the role of gender, academic tenure and earnings', *Scottish Journal of Political Economy*, 53(2), pp. 253–279.

Bennett, S. (2003) 'Flight crew stress and fatigue in low cost commercial air operations – an appraisal', *International Journal of Risk Assessment and Management*, 4(2/3), pp. 207–231.

Bennett, S.A. (2006) *A Sociology of Commercial Flight Crew*, Aldershot: Ashgate.

Blain, A.N.J. (1972) *Pilots and Management*, London: George Allen & Unwin.

Blyton, P. and Turnbull, P. (1992) *Reassessing Human Resource Management*, London: Sage.

Blyton, P. and Turnbull, P. (1995) 'Growing turbulence in the European airline industry', *European Industrial Relations Review*, 255, April, pp. 14–16.

Blyton, P. and Turnbull, P. (1996) 'Confusing convergence: industrial relations in the European airline industry – a comment on Warhurst', *European Journal of Industrial Relations*, 2(1), pp. 7–20.

Blyton, P. and Turnbull, P. (2004) *The Dynamics of Employee Relations* (3rd edn), Basingstoke: Palgrave.

Blyton, P., Martinez Lucio, M., McGurk, J., and Turnbull, P. (1998a) *Globalisation, Deregulation and Flexibility on the Flight Deck*, Report prepared for the European Cockpit Association, Cardiff Business School, Cardiff University.

Blyton, P., Martinez Lucio, M., McGurk, J., and Turnbull, P. (1998b) *Contesting Globalisation: Airline Restructuring, Labour Flexibility and Trade Union Strategies*, London: International Transport Workers' Federation.

Blyton, P., Martinez Lucio, M., McGurk, J., and Turnbull, P. (1999) *Employment Relations Under Deregulation: A Study of European Airlines*, End of Award Report, London: Leverhulme Trust.

Blyton, P., Martinez Lucio, M., McGurk, J., and Turnbull, P. (2001) 'Globalisation and trade union strategy: industrial restructuring and human resource management in the international civil aviation industry', *International Journal of Human Resource Management*, 12(3), pp. 445–463.

Bowey, A. and Thorpe, R. (1986) *Payment Systems and Productivity*, Basingstoke: Macmillan.

Boxall, P. (1996) 'The strategic HRM debate and the resource based view of the firm', *Human Resource Management Journal*, 6(3), pp. 59–75.

Boxall, P. (1998) 'Achieving competitive advantage through human resource management strategy: towards a theory of industry dynamics', *Human Resource Management Review*, 8(3), pp. 265–288.

Boxall, P. (2003) 'HR strategy and competitive advantage in the service sector', *Human Resource Management Journal*, 13(3), pp. 5–20.

Boxall, P. and Purcell, J. (2003) *Strategy and Human Resource Management*, Basingstoke: Palgrave.

Boyd, C. (1999) 'HRM in the airline industry: strategies and outcomes', *Personnel Review*, 30(4), pp. 438–453.

Bratton, J. and Gold, J. (2003) *Human Resource Management: Theory and Practice* (3rd edn), Basingstoke: Palgrave.

Bruch, H. and Sattelberger, T. (2001) 'Lufthansa's transformation marathon: process of liberating and focusing change energy', *Human Resource Management*, 40(3), pp. 249–259.

Bryson, A. (2001) 'Union effects on managerial and employee perceptions of employee relations in Britain', Future of Trade Unions in Modern Britain Programme, Centre for Economic Performance, London School of Economics and Political Science, April.

Bryson, A. (2004) 'Managerial responsiveness to union and non-union voice in Britain', *Industrial Relations*, 43(1), pp. 213–241.

Cappelli, P. (1985) 'Competitive pressures and labour relations in the airline industry', *Industrial Relations*, 24(2), pp. 316–338.

Carson, P.P., Carson, K.D., Birkenmeier, B., and Toma, A.G. (2006) 'Looking for loyalty in all the wrong places: a study of union and organisation commitments', *Public Personnel Management*, 35(2), pp. 137–151.

Cassani, B. and Kemp, K. (2003) *Go: An Airline Adventure*, London: Time Warner.

Child, J. (1972) 'Organization structure, environment and performance: the role of strategic choice', *Sociology*, 6, pp. 1–22.

Child, J. (1988) *Organisations: A Guide to Problems and Practice* (2nd edn), London: Paul Chapman.

Clark, A.E. (1996) 'Job satisfaction in Britain', *British Journal of Industrial Relations*, 34(2), pp. 189–217.

Clugston, M. (2000) 'The mediating effects of multidimensional commitment on job satisfaction and intent to leave', *Journal of Organisational Behaviour*, 21, pp. 477–486.

Colling, T. (1995) 'Experiencing turbulence: competition, strategic choice and the management of human resources in British Airways', *Human Resource Management Journal*, 5(5), pp. 18–32.

Cook, J. and Wall, T. (1980) 'New work attitude measures of trust, organisational commitment and personal need-fulfilment', *Journal of Occupational Psychology*, 53(1), pp. 39–52.

Coulter, A. (2002) 'The year that shook the world', *Travel Trade Gazette*, 2530 (9 September), pp. 26–27.

Cully, M., Woodland, S., O'Reilly, A., and Dix, G. (1999) *Britain at Work*, London: Routledge.

Culpepper, R.A., Gamble, J.E., and Blubaugh, M.G. (2004) 'Employee stock ownership and three-component commitment', *Journal of Occupational & Organizational Psychology*, 77(2), pp. 155–170.

Cutcher-Gershenfeld, J. and Kochan, T. (2004) 'Taking stock: collective bargaining at the turn of the century', *Industrial and Labour Relations Review*, 58(1), pp. 3–26.

Danford, A., Richardson, M., Stewart, P., Tailby, S., and Upchurch, M. (2004) 'High performance work systems and workplace partnership: a case study of aerospace workers', *New Technology, Work and Employment*, 19(1), pp. 14–29.

Danford, A., Richardson, M., Stewart, P., and Upchurch, M. (2005) *Partnership in the High Performance Workplace*, Basingstoke: Palgrave.

Dean, L.R. (1954) 'Union activity and dual loyalty', *Industrial and Labour Relations Review*, 12, pp. 526–536.

Deery, S., (2002) 'Employee reactions to human resource management: a review and assessment', *The Journal of Industrial Relations*, 44(3), pp. 458–466.

Deery, S.J. and Iverson, R.D. (2005) 'Labor–management cooperation: antecedent and impact on organizational performance', *Industrial and Labour Relations Review*, 58(4), pp. 588–609.

Deery, S.J., Iverson, R.D., and Erwin, P.J. (1994) 'Predicting organisational and union commitment: the effect of industrial relations climate', *British Journal of Industrial Relations*, 32(4), pp. 581–597.

Delaney, J.T. and Godard, J. (2001) 'An industrial relations perspective on the high-performance paradigm', *Human Resource Management Review*, 11, pp. 395–429.

Delbridge, R. and Turnbull, P. (1992) 'Human resource maximisation: the management of labour under just-in-time manufacturing systems', in Blyton, P. and Turnbull, P. (eds) *Reassessing Human Resource Management*, London: Sage.

Denzin, N.K. (1970) *The Research Act: A Theoretical Introduction to Sociological Methods*, Chicago: Aldine.

DiMaggio, P. and Powell, W. (1983) 'The iron cage revisited: institutional isomorphism and collective rationality in organizational fields', *American Sociological Review*, 48(2), pp. 147–160.

Doganis, R. (2001) *The Airline Business in the 21st Century*, London: Routledge.

Doganis, R. (2006) *The Airline Business*, London: Routledge.

Eaton, J. (2001) *Globalisation and Human Resource Management in the Airline Industry* (2nd edn), Aldershot: Ashgate.

Edwards, P. and Wright, M. (2001) 'High-involvement work systems and performance outcomes: the strength of variable, contingent and context-bound relationships', *Human Resource Management*, (12)4, June, pp. 568–585.

Eisenberger, R., Huntington, R., Hutchinson, S., and Sowa, D. (1986) 'Perceived organizational support', *Journal of Applied Psychology*, 71, pp. 500–507.

European Cockpit Association (ECA) (2002) 'Upheaval in the European skies', Brussels.

Flin, R. and Martin, L. (2001) 'Behavioural markers for crew resource management: a review of current practice', *The International Journal of Aviation Psychology*, 11(1), pp. 95–118.

Fombrun, C.J., Tichy, N.M., and Devanna, M.A. (1984) *Strategic Human Resource Management*, New York: John Wiley & Sons.

Fontana, A. and Frey, J. (1994) 'Interviewing: the art of science', in Denzin, N. and Lincoln, Y. (eds) *Handbook of Qualitative Research*, Thousand Oaks, Calif.: Sage.

Fowler, F.J. (2002) *Survey Research Methods*, London: Sage.

Frankfort-Nachmias, C. and Nachmias, D. (1996) *Research Methods in the Social Sciences* (5th edn), New York: St Martin's Press.

Freeman, R.B. (1978) 'Job satisfaction as an economic variable', *American Economic Review*, 68, pp. 135–141.

Freeman, R.B. and Medoff, J.L. (1984) *What Do Unions Do?*, New York: Basic Books.

Gallie, D., Felstead, A., and Green, F. (2001) 'Employer policies and organisational commitment in Britain 1992–7', *Journal of Management Studies*, 38(8), pp. 1081–1101.

Gardener, T., Moynihan, L., Park, H., and Wright, P. (2001) 'Beginning to unlock the black box in the HR firm performance relationship: the impact of HR practices on employee attitudes and employee outcomes', Centre for Advanced Human Resource Studies, Cornell University, Working Paper 01–12.

Gazioglu, S. and Tansel, A. (2006) 'Job satisfaction in Britain: individual and job related factors', *Applied Economics*, 38(10), pp. 1163–1171.

Gill, J. and Johnson, P. (1997) *Research Methods for Managers* (2nd edn), London: Sage.

Gittell, J.H. (2003) *The Southwest Airlines Way: Using the Power of Relationships to Achieve High Performance*, New York: McGraw Hill.

Gittell, J., von Nordenflycht, A., and Kochan, T. (2004) 'Mutual gains or zero sum? Labour relations and firm performance in the airline industry', *Industrial and Labour Relations Review*, 57(2), pp. 163–180.

Godard, J. (2001) 'High performance and the transformation of work? The implications of alternative work practices for the experience and outcomes of work', *Industrial and Labour Relations Review*, 54(4), pp. 776–805.

Gordon, M.E., Philpot, J.W., Burt, R.E., Thompson, C.A., and Spiller, W.E. (1980) 'Commitment to the union: development of a measure and examination of its correlates', *Journal of Applied Psychology*, 65, pp. 479–499.

Gouldner, A.W. (1957) 'Cosmopolitans and locals: towards an analysis of latent social roles', *Administrative Science Quarterly*, 2, pp. 281–306.

Granistas, A. and Westlake, M. (2001) 'Cathay goes for broke', *Far Eastern Economic Review*, 164(33), p. 40.

Grant, D. and Shields, J. (2002) 'In search of the subject: researching employee reactions to human resource management', *Journal of Industrial Relations*, 44(3), pp. 313–334.

Grugulis, I. and Wilkinson, A. (2002) 'Managing culture at British Airways: hype, hope and reality', *Long Range Planning*, 35(2), pp. 179–194.

Guest, D.E. (1987) 'Human resource management and industrial relations', *Journal of Management Studies*, 24(5), pp. 503–521.

Guest, D.E. (1989) 'Human resource management: its implications for industrial relations and trade unions', in Storey, J. (ed.) *New Perspectives on Human Resource Management*, London: Routledge.

Guest, D.E. (1995) 'Human resource management, trade unions and industrial relations', in J. Storey, *Human Resource Management: A Critical Text*, London: Routledge.

Guest, D.E. (1999) 'Human resource management – the workers' verdict', *Human Resource Management Journal*, 9(3), pp. 5–25.

Guest, D.E. (2001) 'Industrial relations and human resource management', in Storey, J. (ed.) *Human Resource Management: A Critical Text*, London: Thomson.

Guest, D.E. (2005) 'Human resource management, trade unions and industrial relations', in Salaman, G., Storey, J., and Billsberry, J. (eds) *Strategic Human Resource Management* (2nd edn), London: Sage.

Guest, D.E. and Dewe, P. (1991) 'Company or trade union: which wins workers' allegiance? A study of commitment in the UK electronic industry', *British Journal of Industrial Relations*, 29, pp. 75–96.

Guest, D.E. and Hoque, K. (1996) 'Human resource management and the new industrial relations', in Beardwell, I. (ed.) *Contemporary Industrial Relations: A Critical Analysis*, Oxford: Oxford University Press.

Guest, D.E. and Conway, N. (1999) 'Peering into the black hole: the downside of the new employment relations in the UK', *British Journal of Industrial Relations*, 37(3), pp. 367–389.

Guest, D.E. and Peccei, R. (2001) 'Partnership at work: mutuality and the balance of advantage', *British Journal of Industrial Relations*, 39(2), pp. 207–236.

Harrison, D.A., Newman, D.A., and Roth, P.L. (2006) 'How important are job attitudes? Meta-analytic comparisons of integrative behavioural outcomes and time sequences', *Academy of Management Journal*, 49(2), pp. 305–325.

Harrison, M. (2002) 'bmi transfers East Midlands flights to no-frills unit', *The Independent*, 30 July.

Harvey, G. (2001) 'Militancy and partnership: the development of industrial relations at British Airways', paper presented at the Involvement and Participation Association Assessing Partnership Conference, Leeds University Business School.

Harvey, G. and Turnbull, P. (2002) *Contesting the Crisis: Aviation Industrial Relations and Trade Union Strategies After 11 September*, London: International Transport Workers' Federation.

Hearn, G. (2006) 'Low cost airline, high cost pilots?', *Airfinance Journal*, 289, pp. 46–47.

Hedge, J.W., Bruskiewicz, K.T., Borman, W.C., Hanson, M.A., Logan, K.K., and Siem, F.M. (2000) 'Selecting pilots with crew resource management skills', *The International Journal of Aviation Psychology*, 10(4), pp. 377–392.

Hendry, C., Pettigrew, A.M., and Sparrow, P.R. (1989) 'Linking strategic change, competitive performance and human resource management: results of a UK empirical study', in Mansfield, R. (ed.) *Frontiers of Management Research*, London: Routledge.

Herrbach, O. (2006) 'A matter of feeling? The affective tone of organizational commitment and identification', *Journal of Organizational Behaviour*, 27, pp. 629–643.

Herrbach, O. and Mignonac, K. (2004) 'How organisational image affects employee attitudes', *Human Resource Management Journal*, 14(4), pp. 76–88.

Hirschman, A.O. (1970) *Exit, Voice and Loyalty: Responses to Decline in Firms, Organisations and States*, Cambridge, Mass.: Harvard University Press.

Hoell, R.C. (2004) 'How employee involvement affects union commitment', *Journal of Labour Research*, 19(2), pp. 161–177.

Hope, C. (2002) 'Training scheme no token gesture', *Flight International*, 29 October.

Hopfl, H., Smith, S., and Spencer, S. (1992) 'Values and valuations: the conflicts between culture change and job cuts', *Personnel Review*, 21(1), pp. 24–38.

Hoque, K. (2003) 'All in all, it's just another plaque on the wall: the incidence and impact of the investors in people standard', *Journal of Management Studies*, 40(2), pp. 543–571.

Huselid, M.A. (1995) 'The impact of human resource management practices on turnover, productivity, and corporate financial performance', *Academy of Management Journal*, 38, pp. 635–672.

Hyman, R. (1971) *Marxism and the Sociology of Trade Unionism*, London: Pluto.

Hyman, R. (1975) *Industrial Relations: A Marxist Introduction*, London: Macmillan.

Idson, T.L. (1990) 'Establishment size, job satisfaction and the structure of work', *Applied Economics*, 22, pp. 1007–1018.

Ionides, N., Endres, G., Pilling, M., and Sobie, B. (2007) 'The airline wants YOU', *Airline Business*, 23(1), January, pp. 40–42.

Iverson, R.D. and Buttigieg, D.M. (1999) 'Affective, normative and continuance commitment: can the "right kind" of commitment be managed?', *Journal of Management Studies*, 36(3), pp. 307–333.

Johnson, N.B. (2002) 'Airlines: can collective bargaining weather the storm?', in Clark, P.F., Delaney, J.T., and Frost, A.C. (eds) *Collective Bargaining in the Private Sector*, New York: Cornell University Press.

Johnson, P. and Duberley, J. (2003) 'Reflexivity in management research', *Journal of Management Studies*, 40(5), pp. 1279–1303.

Johnson, R.E and Chang, C.H. (2006) '"I" is to continuance as "we" is to affective: the relevance of the self-concept for organisational commitment', *Journal of Organizational Behaviour*, 27, pp. 549–570.

Johnstone, S., Wilkinson, A., and Ackers, P. (2004) 'Partnership paradoxes: a case study of an energy company', *Employee Relations*, 26(4), pp. 353–376.

Kaufman, B.E. (2003) 'High-level employee involvement at Delta Air Lines', *Human Resource Management*, 42(2), pp. 175–190.

Keenoy, T. (1999) 'HRM as hologram: a polemic', *Journal of Management Studies*, 36(1), pp. 1–23.

Kelly, J. (1996) 'Union militancy and social partnership', in Ackers, P., Smith, C., and Smith, P. (eds) *The New Workplace and Trade Unionism*, London, Routledge.

Kelly, J. (1998) *Rethinking Industrial Relations: Mobilization, Collectivism and Long Waves*, London: Routledge.

Kelly, J. (1999) 'Social partnership in Britain: good for profits, bad for jobs and unions', *Communist Review*, 30(3), pp. 3–10.

Kelly, J. (2004) 'Social partnership agreements in Britain: labour cooperation and compliance', *Industrial Relations*, 43(1), pp. 267–292.

Kinicki, A.J., Carson, K.P., and Bohlander, G.W. (1992) 'Relationship between an organization's human resource efforts and employee attitudes', *Group and Organization Management*, 17, pp. 135–152.

Kinnie, N., Hutchinson, S., Purcell, J., and Swart, J. (2006) 'Human resource management and organisational performance', in Redman, T. and Wilkinson, A. (eds) *Contemporary Human Resource Management* (2nd edn), Harlow: Pearson.

Kochan, T. and Osterman, P. (1994) *The Mutual Gains Enterprise: Forging a Winning Partnership among Labour, Management and Government*, Boston: Harvard Business School Press.

Kochan, T., Katz, H., and McKersie, R.B. (1986) *The Transformation of American Industrial Relations*, New York: Basic Books.

Kochan, T., McKersie, R.B., and Cappelli, P. (1987) 'Strategic choice and industrial relations theory', *Industrial Relations*, 23(1), pp. 16–39.

Kochan, T., von Nordenflycht, A., McKersie, R., and Gittell, J. (2003) 'Out of the ashes: options for rebuilding airline labour relations', Institute for Work and Employment Research (IWER) Working Paper 04–2003.

Korczynski, M. (2002) *Human Resource Management in Service Work*, Basingstoke: Palgrave.

Koys, D.J. (1988) 'Human resource management and a culture of respect: effects on employees' organizational commitment', *Employee Responsibility and Rights Journal*, 1, pp. 57–67.

Koys, D.J. (1991) 'Fairness, legal compliance and organizational commitment', *Employee Responsibility and Rights Journal*, 4, pp. 283–291.

Legge, K. (1995) *Human Resource Management: Rhetorics and Realities*, Basingstoke: Macmillan.

Legge, K. (2001) 'Silver bullet or spent round? Assessing the meaning of the "High commitment management"/performance relationship', in Storey, J. (ed.) *Human Resource Management: A Critical Text* (2nd edn), London: Thomson.

Levitt, S.D. and Dubner, S.J. (2005) *Freakonomics*, London: Penguin.

Locke, E.A. (1976) 'The nature and causes of job satisfaction', in Dunnette, M. (ed.) *The Handbook of Industrial and Organizational Psychology*, Chicago: Rand McNally.

McCartney, S. (2000) 'Pilot shortage siphons experienced instructors from flight schools', *Wall Street Journal – Eastern Edition*, 236(28), p. 1.

McEvoy, G.M. and Cascio, W.F. (1985) 'Strategies for reducing employee turnover: a meta-analysis', *Journal of Applied Psychology*, 70, pp. 342–353.

Machin, S. and Wood, S. (2005) 'Human resource management as a substitute for trade unions in British workplaces', *Industrial and Labour Relations Review*, 58(2), pp. 201–218.

Magenau, J.M., Martin, J.E., and Peterson, M.M. (1988) 'Dual and unilateral commitment among stewards and rank and file union members', *Academy of Management Journal*, 31, pp. 359–376.

Marchington, M. and Grugulis, I. (2000) 'Best practice human resource management: perfect opportunity or dangerous illusion?', *International Journal of Human Resource Management*, 11(6), pp. 1104–1124.

Marks, A., Findlay, P., Hine, J., McKinlay, A., and Thompson, P. (1998) 'The politics of partnership? Innovation in employment relations in the Scottish spirits industry', *British Journal of Industrial Relations*, 36(2), pp. 209–226.

Masters, M.F., Albright, R.R., and Eplion, D. (2006) 'What did partnerships do? Evidence from the federal sector', *Industrial and Labor Relations Review*, 59(3), pp. 367–385.

Merton, R., Fiske, M., and Kendall, P. (1956) *The focused interview: a manual of problems and procedures*, Glencoe, Ill.: Free Press.

Meyer, J.P. and Allen, N.J. (1991) 'A three-component conceptualization of organizational commitment', *Human Resource Management*, 1, pp. 61–89.

Meyer, J.P. and Smith, C.A. (2000) 'HRM practices and organizational commitment: test of a mediation model', *Canadian Journal of Administrative Sciences*, 17(4), pp. 319–331.

Millward, N. (1994) *The New Industrial Relations?*, London: Policy Studies Institute.

Mintzberg, H. (1979) *The Structuring of Organisations: A Synthesis of the Research*, New Jersey: Prentice Hall.

Moorman, R.W. (2000) 'Shortage, what shortage?', *Air Transport World*, 37(8), p. 67.

Moorman, R.W. (2001) 'Perfect storm looms for carriers', *Aviation Week and Space Technology*, 154(2), pp. 32–37.

Murphy, C. and Olthuis, D. (1995) 'The impact of work reorganisation on employee attitudes towards work, the company and the union', in Schenk, C. and Anderson, J. (eds) *Re-shaping Work: Union Responses to Technological Change*, Ontario: Ontario Federation of Labour.

Oppenheim, A.N. (1992) *Questionnaire Design, Interviewing and Attitude Measurement*, London: Continuum.

Oxenbridge, S. and Brown, W. (2002) 'The two faces of partnership? An assessment of partnership and co-operative employer/trade union relations', *Employee Relations*, 24(3), pp. 262–276.

Oxenbridge, S. and Brown, W. (2004) 'Achieving a new equilibrium? The stability of cooperative employer–union relationships', *Industrial Relations Journal*, 35(5), pp. 388–402.

Parker, M. and Slaughter, J. (1988) *Choosing Sides: Unions and the Team Concept*, Boston: South End Press.

Patterson, M., West, M., Lawthorn, R., and Nickell, S. (1997) *The Impact of People Management Practices on Business Performance*, London: Institute of Personnel and Development.

Payne, S.C. and Huffman, A.H. (2005) 'A longitudinal examination of the influence of mentoring on organisational commitment and turnover', *Academy of Management Journal*, 48(1), pp. 158–168.

Penrose, E. (1959) *The Theory of the Growth of the Firm*, Oxford, Blackwell.

Pfeffer, J. (1994) *Competitive Advantage Through People*, Boston: Harvard Business School Press.

Pfeffer, J. (1997) 'Pitfalls on the road to measurement: the dangerous liaison of human resource with the ideas of accounting and finance', *Human Resource Management*, 36(3), pp. 357–365.

Pfeffer, J. (1998) 'Seven practices of successful organisations', *California Management Review*, 40(2), pp. 96–124.

Phillips, E.H. (2003) 'Industry outlook', *Aviation Week & Space Technology*, 158(10), p. 15.

Pilling, M. (2001) 'Leisure market relies on guesswork', *Airline Business*, December.

Pilling, M. (2003) 'Share benefits: pan European leisure travel groups are increasingly looking for ways to share aircraft, flight crew and buying power across their airline subsidiaries', *Flight International*, 29 April, p. 30.

Pilling, M. and Field, D. (2003) 'Pilot performance', *Airline Business*, 1 September, pp. 42–43.

Pollock, L. (2001) 'The bigger easy', *People Management*, 22 March.

Poole, M. (1990) 'Editorial: HRM in an international perspective', *International Journal of Human Resource Management*, 1(1), pp. 1–15.

Porter, L.W., Steers, R.M., Mowday, R.T., and Boulian, R.T. (1974) 'Organizational commitment, job satisfaction and turnover among psychiatric technicians', *Journal of Applied Psychology*, 59, pp. 603–609.

Pudelko, M. (2005) 'Cross national learning from best practice and the convergence–divergence debate in HRM', *International Journal of Human Resource Management*, 16(11), pp. 123–153.

Purcell, J. (1981) *Good Industrial Relations: Theory and Practice*, London: Macmillan.

Purcell, J. (1987) 'Mapping management styles in employment relations', *Journal of Management Studies*, 24(5), pp. 533–548.

Purcell, J. (1999) 'The search for "best practice" or "best fit": chimera or cul-de-sac?', *Human Resource Management Journal*, 9(3), pp. 26–41.

Purcell, J. (2004) 'The HRM–performance link: when, how and why does people management impact on organizational performance?', John Lovett Memorial Lecture, University of Limerick.

Purcell, J., Kinnie, N., Hutchinson, S., Rayton, B., and Stuart, J. (2003) *People and Performance: How People Management Impacts on Organizational Performance*, London: Chartered Institute of Personnel and Development.

Purcell, T.V. (1954) 'Dual allegiance to company and union: packinghouse workers', *Personnel Psychology*, 7, pp. 48–58.

Ramsay, H., Scholarios, D., and Harley, B. (2000) 'Employees and high-performance work systems: testing inside the black box', *British Journal of Industrial Relations*, 38 (4), pp. 501–531.

Rigby, R. (1997) 'Cheap and cheerful', *Management Today*, August, p. 52.

Roche, W.K. and Geary, J.F. (2002) 'Advocates, critics and union involvement in workplace partnership: Irish airports', *British Journal of Industrial Relations*, 40(4), pp. 659–688.

Rousseau, D.M. (1990) 'New hire perceptions of their own and their employers' obligations: a study of psychological contracts', *Journal of Organizational Behaviour*, 11, pp. 389–400.

Sano, Y. (1998) 'Commitment', in Poole, M. and Warner, M. (eds) *The IEBM Handbook of Human Resource Management*, London: Thomson.

Saunders, A. (2002) 'The new skymasters', *Management Today*, September, pp. 44–51.

Scheerhoot, J. (2003) 'Pilots lift threat to holiday flights', *Manchester Evening News*, 13 August.

Schuler, R.S. (1992) 'Strategic human resources management: linking the people with the strategic needs of the business', 21(1), pp. 18–32.

Schuler, R.S. and Jackson, S.E. (1987) 'Linking competitive strategies with human resource management practices', *Academy of Management Executive*, 9(3), pp. 207–219.

Scott, A., Gravelle, H., Simoens, S., Bojke, C., and Sibbald, B. (2006) 'Job satisfaction and quitting intentions: a structural model of British general practitioners', *British Journal of Industrial Relations*, 44(3), pp. 519–540.

Shields, M.A. and Ward, M. (2001) 'Improving nurse retention in the National Health Service in England: the impact of job satisfaction on intentions to quit', *Journal of Health Economics*, 20(5), pp. 677–701.

Sisson, K. (1990) 'Introducing the *Human Resource Management Journal*', *Human Resource Management Journal*, 1(1), pp. 1–11.

Sisson, K. (1993) 'In search of HRM', *British Journal of Industrial Relations*, 31(2), pp. 201–210.

Slocombe, T.E. and Dougherty, T.W. (1998) 'Dissecting organizational commitment and its relationship with employee behaviour', *Journal of Business and Psychology*, 12(4), pp. 469–491.

Sparrow, P., Schuler, R., and Jackson, S. (1994) 'Convergence or divergence: human resource practices and policies for competitive advantage worldwide', *International Journal of Human Resource Management*, 5(2), pp. 267–299.

Spencer, C. (1983) *On the Edge of the Organisation*, Chichester: Wiley.

Storey, J. (1992) *Developments in the Management of Human Resources*, Oxford: Blackwell.

Sull, D. (1999) 'easyJet's $500 million gamble', *European Management Journal*, 17(1), pp. 20–38.

Swailes, S. (2004) 'Commitment to change: profiles of commitment and in-role performance', *Personnel Review*, 33(2), pp. 187–204.

Swiercz, P.M. and Spencer, B.A. (1992) 'HRM and sustainable competitive advantage: lessons from Delta Air Lines', *Human Resource Planning*, 15(2), pp. 35–46.

Thomas, D. (2005) 'Pilot shortage could add to summer woes', *Personnel Today*, 2 August.

Tregaskis, O. and Brewster, C. (2006) 'Converging or diverging? A comparative analysis of trends in contingent employment practice in Europe over a decade', *Journal of International Business Studies*, 37(1), pp. 111–126.

Truss, C. (2001) 'Complexities and controversies in linking HRM with organisational outcomes', *Journal of Management Studies*, 38(8), pp. 1121–1149.

Turnbull, P. and Harvey, G. (2001) *The Impact of 11 September in the Civil Aviation Industry: Social and Labour Effects*, Working Paper No. 182, Geneva: International Labour Office.

Turnbull, P., Blyton, P., and Harvey, G. (2004) 'Cleared for take-off? Management–labour partnership in the European civil aviation industry', *European Journal of Industrial Relations*, 10(3), pp. 287–308.

Von Nordenflycht, A. (2002) 'Alternative approaches to airline labour relations: lessons for the future', Massachusetts Institute of Technology Global Airline Industry Programme.

Wallace, J.E. (1995) 'Organizational and professional commitment in nonprofessional organizations', *Administrative Science Quarterly*, 40, pp. 228–255.

Walton, R. (1985) 'From control to commitment in the workplace', *Harvard Business Review*, 63(2), March–April, pp. 77–84.

Warhurst, R. (1995) 'Converging on HRM? Change and continuity in European airlines' industrial relations', *European Journal of Industrial Relations*, 1(2), pp. 259–274.

Watkins, J. (2003) 'Serious turbulence', *People Management*, 9(16), 7 August, pp. 12–14.

Wayne, S.J., Shore, M., and Liden, R.C. (1997) 'Perceived organizational support and leader–member exchange: a social exchange perspective', *Academy of Management Journal*, 40, pp. 82–111.

Whitener, E.M. (2001) 'Do "high commitment" human resource practices affect employee commitment? A cross-level analysis using hierarchical linear modelling', *Journal of Management*, 27, pp. 515–535.

Wolmar, C. (1996) 'Last call for the captains in blue', *Independent*, 9 July.

Wood, S. (1999) 'Getting the measure of the transformed high performance organization', *British Journal of Industrial Relations*, 37(3), pp. 391–417.

Wood, S. and Albanese, M. (1995) 'Can we speak of high commitment management on the shop floor?', *Journal of Management Studies*, 32(2), pp. 215–247.

Wright, E.O. (2000) 'Working-class power, capitalist-class interests, and class compromise', *American Journal of Sociology*, 105(4), pp. 957–1002.

Wright, P.M. and Boswell, W.R. (2002) 'Desegregating HRM: a review and synthesis of micro and macro human resource management research', *Journal of Management*, 28(3), pp. 247–276.

Wright, P., Gardener, T., Moynihan, L., and Park, H. (2001) 'Measurement error in research of human resources and firm performance: additional data and suggestions for future research', *Personnel Psychology*, 54(4), pp. 875–901.

Wright, P., McMahon, G., and McWilliams, A. (1994) 'Human resources and sustained competitive advantage: a resource-based perspective', *International Journal of Human Resource Management*, 5(2), pp. 301–326.

Zhou, J. and George, J.M. (2001) 'When job dissatisfaction leads to creativity: encouraging the expression of voice', *Academy of Management Journal*, 44(4), pp. 682–696.

# Index

Tables are indicated by *italic* page numbers, figures by **bold** numbers.

normative commitment 96

older workers and job satisfaction 76
**one**world 15, 63
organisational commitment: benefits of
    95–6; four bases of 96; and HRM
    96–104; HRM style as influential
    factor 104; as indicator of HRM
    impact 31–2; involvement and
    participation of employees 96–7,
    101–2; questionnaire survey 98–100,
    *100*; and rank 103, *104*; and
    satisfaction with salary 102–3, *103*;
    and union commitment 104–8, *106*,
    *107*, *108*, 128
organisational support 33–4
Osterman, P. 111–12
out-basing 15–16, 21
outsourcing 20, 21
Oxenbridge, S. 38

partnership 37–9; advocates of 111–12;
    attitude of unions towards 110,
    111–13; Britannia Airways 116;
    British Airways 115–16, 116–19;
    components of 111; critics of
    112–13; and incorporation theory
    112; pilots attitudes to 114–23, *115*,
    *118*, *120*, 129; and power of pilots
    113–14; and professionalism of
    pilots 114; Scottish spirits industry
    112; trade unions' efficacy under
    118–23, *120*, *121*, 129–30; union
    patronage of 114
Patterson, M., West, M., Lawthorn, R.
    and Nickell, S. 25
Payne, J. 38, 111
Penrose, E. 25
Perry, J.L. 105
pilots: attitudes to partnership 114–23,
    *115*, *118*, *120*, 129; challenge to
    work routines of 7–8; costs to qualify
    as 8; deskilling of 7; impact of
    September 11 attacks 23, 90–4, *91*,
    *92*, *93*; impact on of industry
    changes 20–1; industrial power of
    8–9; lack of alternative employment
    10; and low-cost airlines 17–20, **19**;
    organisation of work at easyJet 57–8,
    *58*; organisational and union

commitment of *106*, 106–8, *107*,
    *108*, 128; and organisational
    commitment and HRM 98–104;
    perception of impact of 9/11 90–4,
    *91*, *92*, *93*; power of 113–14;
    professionalism of 114; recognition
    of HRM content 50–4, *52*;
    relationships with management *86*,
    86–9; resistance to restructuring 21;
    selection of for survey 46; and the
    seniority clause 10–11; status of
    83–6, *84*; work-to-rule 12
policies and practices of HRM 24–6,
    44, *45*
Pollock, L. 56
Powell, W. 34–5
privatisation of airlines 15
problem-solving groups 53–4
professionals and job satisfaction 75
Purcell, J. 27, 28–9, 31; *see also*
    Kinnie, N., Hutchinson, S., Purcell,
    J. and Swart, J.

questionnaire survey 43–8, *45*, *47*

Ramsey, H., Scholarios, D. and Harley,
    B. 32
rank and job satisfaction 78, *78*, 82,
    *82*
*Reassessing Human Resource
    Management* (Blyton and Turnbull)
    24
reflexivity 41
research project: data analysis 48;
    exploratory interviews 41–2, *42*;
    focus groups 43; questionnaire
    survey 43–8, *45*; sample airlines 50;
    secondary data analysis 40
resource-based theory of the firm 25
response rate for survey 46–8, *47*
rosters 89–90, *90*
Ryanair 16

salaries: and job satisfaction *83*, 78–9,
    *79*, 82–3; and organisational
    commitment 102–3, *103*
sample airlines 50
Scholarios, D. *see* Ramsey, H.,
    Scholarios, D. and Harley, B.
Scottish spirits industry 112